**P9-CDF-159**

Empowering Women and Men to Use Their Gifts Together in Advancing the Gospel

Occasional Paper No. 53

Produced by the Issue Group on this topic at the 2004 Forum

hosted by the

Lausanne Committee for World Evangelization

In Pattaya, Thailand, September 29 to October 5, 2004

"A New Vision, a New Heart and a Renewed Call"

Lausanne Occasional Paper (LOP) No.53
This Issue Group on Empowering women and men to use their
gifts together in advancing the gospel was Issue Group No.24
(there were 31 Issue Groups at the Forum)

Series Editor for the 2004 Forum Occasional Papers (commencing
with LOP 30): David Claydon

The context for the production of the Lausanne Occasional Papers

The Lausanne Movement is an international movement committed to energising **"the whole Church to take the whole gospel to the whole world"**.

With roots going back to the historical conferences in Edinburgh (1910) and Berlin (1966), the Lausanne Movement was born out of the First International Congress on World Evangelization called by evangelist Billy Graham held in Lausanne, Switzerland, in July 1974. The landmark outcome of this Congress was the *Lausanne Covenant* supported by the 2430 participants from 150 nations. The covenant declares the substance of the Christian faith as historically declared in the creeds and adds a clear missional dimension to our faith. Many activities have emerged from the Lausanne Congress and from the second congress held in Manila in 1989. The Covenant (in a number of languages) and details about the many regional events and specialised conferences which have been undertaken in the name of Lausanne may be examined on the website at www.lausanne.org .

The continuing Lausanne International Committee believed it was led by the Holy Spirit to hold another conference which would bring together Christian leaders from around the world. This time the Committee planned to have younger emerging leaders involved and sought funds to enable it to bring a significant contingent from those parts of the world where the church is rapidly growing today. It decided to call the conference a **Forum.** As a Forum its structure would be to allow people to come and participate if they had something to contribute to one of 31 issues. These issues were chosen through a global research programme seeking to identify the most significant issues in the world today which are of concern in our task to take the *good news* to the world.

This Lausanne Occasional Paper (LOP) is the report which has emerged from one of these Issue Groups. LOPs have been produced for each of the Issue Groups and information regarding these and other publications may be obtained by going to the website at www.lausanne.org .

The theme of the Forum for World Evangelization held in 2004 was **"A new vision, a new heart and a renewed call"**. This Forum was held in Pattaya, Thailand from September 29 to October 5, 2004. 1530 participants came from 130 countries to work in one of the 31 Issue Groups.

The Affirmations at the conclusion of the Forum stated:
There has been a spirit of working together in serious dialogue and prayerful reflection. Representatives from a wide spectrum of cultures and virtually all parts of the world have come together to learn from one another and to seek new direction from the Holy Spirit for world evangelization. They committed themselves to joint action under divine guidance.

The dramatic change in the political and economic landscape in recent years has raised new challenges in evangelization for the church. The polarization between east and west makes it imperative that the church seek God's direction for the appropriate responses to the present challenges.

In the 31 Issue Groups these new realities were taken into consideration, including the HIV pandemic, terrorism, globalization, the global role of media, poverty, persecution of Christians, fragmented families, political and religious nationalism, post-modern mind set, oppression of children, urbanization, neglect of the disabled and others.

Great progress was made in these groups as they grappled for solutions to the key challenges of world evangelization. As these groups focused on making specific recommendations, larger strategic themes came to the forefront.

There was affirmation that major efforts of the church must be directed toward those who have no access to the gospel. The commitment to help establish self sustaining churches within 6000 remaining unreached people groups remains a central priority.

Secondly, the words of our Lord call us to love our neighbour as ourselves. In this we have failed greatly. We renew our commitment to reach out in love and compassion to those who are marginalised because of disabilities or who have different lifestyles and spiritual perspectives. We commit to reach out to children and young people who constitute a majority of the world's population, many of whom are being abused, forced into slavery, armies and child labour.

A third stream of a strategic nature acknowledges that the growth of the church is now accelerating outside of the western world. Through the participants from Africa, Asia and Latin America, we recognise the dynamic nature and rapid growth of the church in the *South*. Church leaders from the *South* are increasingly providing exemplary leadership in world evangelization.

Fourthly, we acknowledge the reality that much of the world is made up of oral learners who understand best when information comes to them by means of stories. A large proportion of the world's populations are either unable to or unwilling to absorb information through written communications. Therefore, a need exists to share the "Good News" and to disciple new Christians in story form and parables.

Fifthly, we call on the church to use media to effectively engage the culture in ways that draw non believers toward spiritual truth and to proclaim Jesus Christ in culturally relevant ways.

Finally, we affirm the priesthood of all believers and call on the church to equip, encourage and empower women, men and youth to fulfil their calling as witnesses and co-labourers in the world wide task of evangelization.

Transformation was a theme which emerged from the working groups. We acknowledge our own need to be continually transformed, to continue to open ourselves to the leading of the Holy Spirit, to the challenges of God's word and to grow in Christ together with fellow Christians in ways that result in social and economic transformation. We acknowledge that the scope of the gospel and building the Kingdom of God involves, body, mind, soul and spirit. Therefore we call for increasing integration of service to society and proclamation of the gospel.

We pray for those around the world who are being persecuted for their faith and for those who live in constant fear of their lives. We uphold our brothers and sisters who are suffering. We recognize that the reality of the persecuted church needs to be increasingly on the agenda of the whole body of Christ. At the same time, we also acknowledge the importance of loving and doing good to our enemies while we fight for the right of freedom of conscience everywhere.

We are deeply moved by the onslaught of the HIV/AIDS pandemic – the greatest human emergency in history. The Lausanne movement calls all churches everywhere to prayer and holistic response to this plague.

"9/11", the war in Iraq, the war on terror and its reprisals compel us to state that we must not allow the gospel or the Christian faith to be captive to any one geo-political entity. We affirm that the Christian faith is above all political entities.

We are concerned and mourn the death and destruction caused by all conflicts, terrorism and war. We call for Christians to pray for peace, to be proactively involved in reconciliation and avoid all attempts to turn any conflict into a religious war. Christian mission in this context lies in becoming peace makers.

We pray for peace and reconciliation and God's guidance in how to bring about peace through our work of evangelization. We pray for God to work in the affairs of nations to open doors of opportunity for the gospel. We call on the church to mobilize every believer to focus specific consistent prayer for the evangelization of their communities and the world.

In this Forum we have experienced the partnership of men and women working together. We call on the church around the world to work towards full partnership of men and women in the work of world evangelism by maximising the gifts of all.

We also recognize the need for greater intentionality in developing future leaders. We call on the church to find creative ways to release emerging leaders to serve effectively.

Numerous practical recommendations for local churches to consider were offered. These will be available on the Lausanne website and in the Lausanne Occasional Papers. It is our prayer that these many case studies and action plans will be used of God to mobilize the church to share a clear and relevant message using a variety of methods to reach the most neglected or resistant groups so that everyone will have the opportunity to hear the gospel message and be able to respond to this good news in faith.

We express our gratitude to the Thai Church which has hosted us and to their welcoming presentation to the Forum. We are profoundly gratefully to God for the privilege of being able to gather here from the four corners of the earth. We have developed new partnerships, made new friends and encouraged one another in our various ministries. Not withstanding the resistance to the gospel in many places and the richness of an inherited religious and cultural tradition we here at the Forum have accepted afresh the renewed call to be obedient to the mandate of Christ. We commit ourselves to making His saving love known so that the whole world may have opportunity to accept God's gift of salvation through Christ.

These affirmations indicate the response of the participants to the Forum outcomes and their longing that the whole church may be motivated by the outcomes of the Forum to strengthen its determination to be obedient to God's calling.

May the case studies and the practical suggestions in this and the other LOPs be of great help to you and your church as you seek to find new ways and a renewed call to proclaim the saving love of Jesus Christ.

David Claydon

This Occasional Paper was prepared by the whole Issue Group and
the principal editor was Alvera Mickelsen

CONTENTS

I. ACKNOWLEDGEMENTS
by Mimi Haddad, Convener

More than at any other time in history, Christians around the globe today are rigorously examining what the Bible says regarding gender. As a result, we observe a burgeoning of literature and great discussion at a global level. The Lausanne 2004 Forum for World Evangelization provided nearly 50 Christian leaders from over a dozen countries the opportunity to exchange ideas and determine ways that men and women might work together to advance the gospel in church, home and society.

Our Issue Group, aptly entitled "Empowering Women and Men to Use Their Gifts Together in Advancing the Gospel," engaged in months of online dialogue, and the preparation of the individual papers that were then presented in Thailand. We assessed ministry from a biblical, theological, historical, socio/psychological and missiological perspective. We then asked probing questions as to whether ministry is gift-based, rather than gender-based. We also engaged the prevalent issue of abuse and offered strategies for addressing and preventing physical, emotional and sexual abuse.

When we arrived in Thailand, we observed the Spirit at work in our issue group, as participants spoke boldly on behalf of their biblical convictions and ministry experiences. In the process, we made lifelong friends and are continuing our work together through publications, task groups and conferences.

As convener of Issue Group 24, I would like to thank the Lausanne Committee for the opportunity to explore the important issue of gender. I thank, also, our distinguished delegates whose names appear at the end of this paper. Each delegate made a significant contribution, and while many were unable to attend, their prayers and online contributions served to guide and nourish our work.

Many thanks go to Alvera Mickelsen for her wise, patient and expert service as editor of our Occasional Paper. We greatly appreciate Karen Maczka who served our group so graciously in Thailand. I wish to also thank Mary Gonsior for her expert technical help in assembling the final draft. Jane Crane helped organize this Occasional Paper, for which we are thankful. We are indebted also to Lorry Lutz who served not only as co-convener, but also as a mentor and friend.

1

We pray that the work of Issue Group 24 will, by God's grace, provide new vision and understanding for the equal dignity, service and worth of men and women in ministry.

II. PREFACE
Lausanne and Gender
by Jane Crane

After two years of research, the Lausanne Committee identified thirty-one roadblocks to world evangelism, one of which was the need to empower men and women to use their gifts together in advancing the gospel. The focus on gender was a natural progression. Through Lausanne's worldwide gatherings, over the last thirty years, the topic of gender has been emerging in increasing depth.

The historic Lausanne Covenant of 1979, signed by many leaders and still used across the world, cites gender within the context of social responsibility. This document suggests that Christians are called to share God's "concern for justice and reconciliation throughout human society and for the liberation of men and women from every kind of injustice. Because men and women are made in the image of God, every person, regardless of race, religion, colour, culture, class, sex or age, has an intrinsic dignity because of which he or she should be respected and served, not exploited."

The Manila Manifesto, produced 10 years later in 1989, addressed gender more specifically in two of its 21 "Affirmations:"
- Affirmation #13: "We affirm that we who claim to be members of the Body of Christ must transcend within our fellowship the barriers of race, gender and class."
- Affirmation #14: "We affirm that the gifts of the Spirit are distributed to all God's people, women and men, and that their partnership in evangelization must be welcomed for the common good."

Further, The Manila Manifesto states that women "must be given opportunities to exercise their gifts" and called for suitable training for both men and women. The Manifesto deplored "the failures in Christian consistency," including "sexual discrimination," and affirmed that "co-operation in evangelism is indispensable," with "both sexes working together."

As the 2004 Forum for World Evangelization drew to a close, "Summary Affirmations" were released with a significant statement on gender, which reads: "In this Forum we have experienced the partnership of men and women working together. We call on the church around the

3

world to work towards full partnership of men and women in the work of world evangelization by maximizing the gifts of all."

This Occasional Paper, written by the 2004 Forum's Issue Group 24: "Empowering Women and Men to Use Their Gifts Together in Advancing the Gospel," addresses the foundations for men and women in ministry-partnerships. Our Occasional Paper begins with a Declaration made to the entire Lausanne 2004 Forum, in Thailand. We have also proposed action steps to engage the spiritual gifts of women and men in service to Christ. Finally, we offer research papers that provide a biblical, theological, historical, sociological and missiological basis for empowering men and women's shared ministry.

We anticipate additional strategies will emerge as Christians around the globe continue to recognize the importance of engaging the gifts of women and men who work in full partnership in advancing the gospel of Jesus Christ.

III. ISSUE GROUP 24 DECLARATION

In order that the whole Church may take the whole gospel to the whole world, we, the issue Lausanne Issue Group 24 "Empowering Men and Women for Ministry," affirm that more labourers, both men and women, must be released to exercise their God-given gifts for ministry and leadership. More than half of the body of Christ are women who are the most undervalued and under utilized resource of the Church.

At this critical time the Church urgently needs to empower the ministry of women and men in full partnership. We recognize that the Bible teaches that women and men are equally:

- Created in God's image and likeness and entrusted with dominion.
- Redeemed through the death of Christ.
- Gifted for ministry by the Holy Spirit.
- Called to ministry and servant leadership.
- Held responsible for using their gifts to advance the Kingdom of God.

As the Church we need to:

- Repent of anything that devalues women or men.
- Embrace the teaching and example of Jesus regarding women and the Spirit- given basis for all ministry.
- Affirm the biblical basis for the equal value of men and women in advancing the gospel.
- Pray that God will break the barriers that inhibit ministry and build bridges that enable authentic partnership.
- Model, promote and celebrate mutuality in ministry.
- Invest resources that advance gift-based rather than gender-based ministry.

IV. ACTION STEPS FOR THE CHURCH

The leadership for the Lausanne Forum 2004 has requested that each issue group provide practical challenges for local churches. In light of Issue Group 24's Declaration and the realization that women, in terms of their gifts, are the most underutilized resource of the church, the following steps are suggested. While we recognize that different churches may take different positions, we call upon every church to explore the issues in light of current biblical research. This Occasional Paper, including the "Further Reading" section at the end, offers a wealth of material towards this endeavour.

Local Churches are encouraged to:
1. Establish a "Gender Study Group" who will:
    a. Review the pertinent Scriptures along with historical and theological research of the last two decades.
    b. Examine church leadership including deacons, elders, board membership, Adult Education, evangelism, standing committees etc. Are the gifts of women included?
    c. Examine Church curriculum asking will it empower the gifts of all believers?
    d. Where change is desired, review change dynamics and offer suggestions for gradual transitions where needed.
    e. Report to church leadership how to make ministry gift-based rather than gender-based.
    f. Report progress the Church and to LCWE and or Issue Group 24.

2. Ensure Sunday School classes include God's gifts and call of women as well as men throughout Scripture and history, especially Jesus' treatment of women given the culture of His day.

3. Establish an annual "Domestic Violence Awareness Day." Tackle the subject head-on in a sermon, adult education, curriculum and distribute materials on local resources. Take a special offering and engage in intercessory prayer for ministries that are combating the abuse of women in other countries in Christ's name, such as wife burning in India or the prostitution of young girls (and boys) in Asia.

4. Establish and observe an annual "Worldwide Gender Awareness Day" in March that celebrates the partnerships of men and women in evangelism and ministry.

5. Challenge men and women to empower one another in ministry and to pray for one another.

6. Implement team projects for women and men to learn to use their gifts together.

7. Commit to pray for God to empower men and women to use their gifts to advance Christ's kingdom.

Serving the Church

The Issue Group 24 will continue to address and develop:
1. Curriculum/Literature /Future Publications
   a. A Gender Task Force will consider developing publications to advance women and men in ministry-partnerships.
   b. Develop curriculum for Sunday School classes and small groups.
   c. Distribute and publish the Issue Group 24 Occasional Paper as widely as possible.
   d. Widely distribute and publish the online papers as well as the papers presented in Thailand, 2004.

2. Models
   a. Develop a directory of individuals to be available to speak on the subject.
   b. Develop a directory of men and women in ministry partnerships to be available to speak.

3. Abuse
   a. Network agencies focusing on abuse.
   b. Make information about these agencies available.
   c. Consider future conferences and publications that expand an awareness and prevention of abuse.

4. Create a working task force growing out of the members of Issue Group 24. The working task force will continue to meet and advance the purposes of Issue Group 24 through:
   a. Developing a network of churches and organizations to promote mutuality between men and women in ministry.

b. The Task Force will provide strategies, publications, and other resource to equip churches/organizations in promoting the partnership of men and women in ministry.
c. The Task Force: Will develop strategies, events and publications that advance and expand the work of Issue Group 24 over the next five years.

5. Communications
    a. Web site:
        i.   Develop a Web site to link participating organizations.
        ii. Post the Issue Group 24 Occasional Paper and make it available to other Web sites.
        iii. Develop an Issue Group 24 Web site.
    b. Communicate with Issue 24 participants.
        i.   Prayer requests.
        ii. Opportunities for ministry or training.
        iii. Implementation of future strategies.

Issue Group 24 calls upon Lausanne to consider the following actions:
1. Prayer: Issue Group 24 petitions the Lausanne International prayer team to pray for men and women in ministry.

2. Issue Group 24 petitions Lausanne to include the mutuality of men and women in ministry in all key documents and in future events.

3. We request that other Lausanne issues groups such as "Future Leadership" and the "Church of the Future" engage the work of Issue Group 24 in their study and discussion.

4. We likewise request at the Lausanne Younger Leaders' Conference in 2006 that there be a consideration of empowering young men and women in their calling to take the gospel to the world.

V. RESEARCH PAPERS

1. God's Gifting and Gender

A. What Does Jesus Teach Us About Gender?
Adapted from: "I Commend To You Our Sister"
by David Joel Hamilton

When we look at the teachings of Jesus, it is important that we imagine their impact on his first audience, who lived in a culture entirely different from our own. When compared to what was considered normal for how men and women related to each other in first century Israel, Jesus' words and actions were truly revolutionary.[i]

Jesus' mission was not gender-biased; it was gender-inclusive. Let's look at the way Jesus' ministry transformed the lives of women. What he modelled and taught was totally different from the way women were usually treated in a male-centred world. For Jesus, there was

- no double standard
- no exclusion
- no limits on their God-given destiny

No Double Standard
Jesus refused to adopt the cultural double standard of the day. One example is the story of the woman caught in adultery. Obviously a woman cannot commit adultery by herself, but because the religious leaders held to a double standard they did not bring the man to trial. In the biblical law that Jesus' accusers were supposedly upholding, both the man and the woman were to be put to death. Jesus refused to be pulled into their biased judgment. He quietly wrote on the ground and simply said, "If any of you is without sin, let him be the first to throw a stone at her."[ii]

Jesus' words spoke volumes: sin was sin — whether committed by a man or a woman. When equity is the standard, stones are rarely thrown.

---

[i] David Hamilton and Loren Cunningham, <u>Why Not Women</u>? (YWAM Publishing, 2000)
[ii] John 8:3-11

Jesus' teachings on marriage and divorce were another area where the double standard of the day was discarded. His statements affirmed that women had rights and responsibilities equal to men's. This contrasted sharply with rabbinical thought, where the right of betrothal and divorce belonged exclusively to men.

When the Pharisees brought up the subject of divorce, Jesus directed their thinking back to the equality of men and women in creation.[iii] Then he reminded them that God had said, "For this reason, a man will leave his father and mother and be united to his wife."[iv] The man was told to relinquish the rights to *his* family in order to enter into marriage with *her*. This was unheard of in a world where only women were expected to relinquish rights.

Jesus went on to quote, ". . . and the two will be become one flesh." The Hebrew word *one* is the same word used in Deut. 6:4: "The Lord our God, the Lord is one." The unity that God intended between a husband and wife was to be like the unity that God the Father, God the Son, and God the Holy Spirit have enjoyed for eternity. This is part of the significance of the statement: "Let us make. . . in our image. . . male and female." Since there is no hierarchy in the Trinity, no superior or inferior, there cannot be any between a husband and a wife.

No Exclusion
Jesus refused to follow the common practices that excluded women from meaningful participation in their faith.

Before ascending into heaven, He gave a new sacrament that would include both males and females. The old sacrament, circumcision, was only for males. Baptism, the new rite, was to give both men and women the opportunity to declare their faith publicly.

Another strategy he employed was to include women in his public teaching. He did so even though most Jews considered it improper, even obscene, to teach the Scriptures to women. Jesus' actions show his determination to stop such discrimination. Jesus made a point to do his public teaching in places where women could participate. For example, he often taught in open fields around the Sea of Galilee. When

---

[iii] Genesis 1:26-28
[iv] Genesis 2: 24

Jesus taught in the temple in Jerusalem, it was in the areas that were open to both men and women.[v]

Jesus also taught women in private settings. One occurs in Luke 10:38-42 at the home of Mary, Martha, and Lazarus. Mary "sat at the Lord's feet listening to what he said." That was a common expression pointing to a formal mentoring relationship between a rabbi and his disciple.[vi] In contrast to Jesus' practice, rabbinical teachings said, "He that talks much with womankind brings evil upon himself."[vii] But Jesus defied that rabbinical instruction and defended Mary's right to learn as his disciple. He said, "Mary has chosen what is better and it will not be taken away from her."

At the time of Lazarus' death, Jesus privately engaged Martha in one of the most significant, thought-provoking dialogues in the Gospels, ending with Jesus' declaration, *"I am the resurrection and the life. He who believes in me will live, even though he dies, and whoever lives and believes in me will never die."*[viii] This cornerstone of our faith was revealed to a woman; it is never recorded as being spoken to the 12 disciples. The only way we know of it today is she faithfully passed Jesus' teaching on to others who in turned passed them on to us.

Jesus' conversation with the Samaritan woman at the well[ix] is the longest of his recorded private conversations. She was an outcast to both Jews and Samaritans, yet Jesus engaged her in serious, theological discussion. As a result, this Samaritan woman had an understanding that Jesus was the Christ, the Saviour of the world – long before Peter's similar revelation.[x] When the disciples returned from their visit to the nearby city, their surprise at seeing Jesus talking with a woman exposed their male-centred perspective. Jesus' command to them, *"Lift up your eyes and look,"* was Jesus' way of telling them that their world view was too small! While they were still worrying about lunch, the woman rushed off to become the first evangelist in Samaria!

---

[v] John 8:20; 10:23

[vi] Compare Paul's use of this same phrase used to describe his relationship with Gamaliel (Acts 22:3)

[vii] Mishnah Avot 1.5

[viii] John 11:20-27

[ix] John 4:4-42

[x] John 4: 29, 42. Compare with Mark 8:39

No Limits to God-given Destiny

Jesus refused to put any limit on women being able to fulfil their God-given destiny. His choice to invite only male disciples has been used by some to argue that He was modelling that only males should be involved in ministry. But one could equally point out that the 12 were all ethnic Jews, all Aramaic-speaking and all but Judas were Galilean. If one were to pattern contemporary church leadership on these traits of the disciples, then only Galilean Jews who speak Aramaic should be leaders of the church! Obviously, no one would make this application. So why do so in the gender category?

In a related line of reasoning, some argue that Jesus' use of the term "Father" implies that God is masculine and therefore only males are qualified to lead based on God's own model. This is simply not the case. Jesus' use of the term Father was not designed to communicate about God's gender, but about a new degree of intimacy of relationship He was opening to us through Emmanuel. His use of this word would have been shocking for the Jews of his day, for it was rare for the term "Father" to be used for God in the Old Testament.[xi] Jesus introduced this novel term to show how intimate God wanted to be with people.

At least twice, Jesus spoke of God using feminine terminology — in the parable of the woman searching for a lost coin, and in the parable of a woman hiding yeast in a loaf.[xii] Jesus felt comfortable in using both male and female metaphors for God because God is neither male nor female. In fact, Jesus said that in heaven we would neither marry nor be given in marriage — gender distinctions will be either non-existent or irrelevant. Therefore we cannot disqualify women from leadership and ministry roles that impact eternity based upon gender distinctions which have only a limited temporal duration.

Having discounted a "male only" model of leadership we should ask: did Jesus allow women to minister? Yes. Women ministered both *to* and *with* Jesus. The verb *diakoneo* associated with seven women in the Gospel narratives is the same verb used of seven men appointed to leadership in the early church. This term is used of Peter's mother-in-law; Mary Magdalene; Mary, the mother of James and Joses; Salome, the

---

[xi] While Jesus referred to God as Father 189 times, such terminology was used only 19 times in the Old Testament: Deuteronomy 32:6; 2 Samuel 7:14; 1 Chronicles 17:3; 22:10; 28:6; 29:10; Psalms 68:5; 89:26; 103:13; Proverbs 3: 12; Isaiah 9:6; 63: 16a, 16b; 64:8; Jeremiah 3:4, 19; 31: 9; Malachi 1:6; 2:10
[xii] Luke 13:20-21, 15:8-10

mother of Zebedee's sons; Joanna, the wife of Cuza; Susanna; Martha, sister of Mary and Lazarus.[xiii]

Luke 8:1-3 also tells us that some women regularly travelled with Jesus as part of His ministry team. Jesus' inclusion of them was unheard of in His day and strongly affirmed their right to participate in any ministry role.

Jesus not only permitted women to participate in ministry, but He commanded them to assume public ministry roles. Mary Magdalene and "the women" who were at His tomb were all directly commanded to go and "*tell My brothers I am returning to My Father*"[xiv] and "*tell [them] to go to Galilee where they will see me,*"[xv] respectively. If He trusted them to preach to the apostles, surely He would call all women to proclaim the good news of His resurrection everywhere! How then can we keep women from preaching the gospel when Jesus trusted them with the first proclamation of the resurrection?

There is one other startling encounter that definitively illustrates Jesus' mandate for women's participation in ministry.[xvi] As He was teaching, a woman called out, "*Blessed is she who bore you.*" Her statement reflected the commonly held view that a woman was ascribed honour only through the achievement of her male offspring. Jesus counters with the statement, "*Blessed rather are those who hear the word of God and obey it.*" He clearly affirms that men *and* women are blessed when they step out in obedience to *whatever* God is asking them to do; women are no longer limited to the vicarious praise earned by association with a male family member.

Jesus systematically rejected the system of thought that for centuries had cut women off from active participation in the things of God. He championed their right to be his disciples, engaged them in serious theological discussion and commissioned them to preach the gospel. He affirmed their right to obey the will of God in whatever form of activity that involved, to merit their own commendation for their own steps of faith and obedience. Truly, in all he modelled and spoke, he

---

xiii Matthew 8:14; 27:55-56; Luke 8:3
xiv Mark 16:9-11
xv Matthew 28: 9-10
xvi Luke 11:27

lived a life affirming the right of women to fully participate in seeking and serving God.

B. Does Gender Matter in Advancing the Gospel?
By Alvera Mickelsen

As believers in Christ, we all deeply desire to see the message of the gospel proclaimed and accepted around the world. If we have experienced the power of the Holy Spirit to transform our lives to make us better and more useful persons, we want to let the whole world share that experience.

Jesus tells us in Matthew 28:18 that we are to *"go and make disciples of all nations, baptizing them in the name of the Father and the Son and the Holy Spirit. Teach these new disciples to obey all the commands I have given you."* (Living Translation)

Who is to do this work? Apparently all believers — men and women — are to share this responsibility. A quick look at history indicates that God uses whoever is willing to be used — without regard to gender. However, tradition and culture around the world have often limited the work that women have been permitted or encouraged to do.

The Bible says clearly in Genesis 1 that men and women alike are made in the "image of God" and are given identical responsibilities:
- Be fruitful and multiply.
- Fill the earth and subdue it.
- Have dominion over every living thing.

When sin entered the world (Genesis 3), this oneness and mutuality was damaged and life became much more difficult. Violence, suspicion, and prejudice grew and grew. Power became a consuming desire. This is apparent throughout the Old Testament.

In spite of this, God kept using people (men and women) to carry out His work. We all know about the prophets Moses, Isaiah, Daniel, Ezekiel and others. However, many people have never heard of the prophets Miriam, Deborah and Huldah. We know about King David, but God also used Queen Esther. Gender distinctions were apparently far

14

more important to people than to God. Thus we see God releasing women for service for God, whereas culture restricted them.

This has been true throughout the history of the church and the history of missions.

Although God clearly created and commissioned Adam and Eve as equal partners in the garden, by the time of Jesus, Jewish and Gentile cultures had made women second class citizens with clear limitations on their activities. Nevertheless, Jesus (God in human form) often went contrary to these cultural limitations. He taught women as well as men — not just in crowds, but in more intimate circles as well. Jesus privately taught his disciples that He would be crucified and rise from the dead, (they did not believe it), but we know from Luke 24:6-9 that He also taught about his coming death and resurrection to some of the women who followed Him closely. The angel at the tomb of Jesus reminded the women of what Jesus had taught them — and they remembered his teaching.

Two other examples illustrate Jesus' giving women a place of prominence not granted by the culture at that time. It was to the Samaritan woman at the well that Jesus *first* said to anyone that He was the promised Messiah.

The "bent-over" woman was called to the front of the synagogue (where women were not supposed to go) to be healed by Jesus. (Luke 13:10 - 17)

We also find that women were active leaders of the early church. Before Paul's conversion on the road to Damascus, he was intent on destroying the new followers of "the Way." Acts 8:3 says that Saul was going everywhere to devastate the church. He went from house to house, dragging out both men and women to throw them into jail. Obviously he would not have bothered with women if they had not been important in the burgeoning church.

The first convert and apparent leader of a house church in Greece was Lydia, a seller of purple (Acts 16: 13 - 40).

Women and men prayed and prophesied in the early church (1 Corinthians 11:4, 5). Paul calls Junia a prominent apostle (Romans 16:7).

Paul's favourite co-workers were probably Priscilla and Aquila — a husband and wife team. Paul mentions them more often in the New Testament than anyone except Timothy. Usually, Priscilla's name is mentioned first, (contrary to ancient custom), which probably indicates that she was more the leader of the team.

When intense persecution began against the early church, women where thrown to the lions along with the men.

Women's prominence continued throughout the early church. Women served as missionaries, martyrs, and Bible translators.

In the medieval church, women were often considered inferior, the cause of men's sin, and restricted from most church ministries. During this period convents and monasteries were common place and women were always in charge of convents. Such women include Hildegard of Bingen (11th century). Hildegard was Abbess of a double monastery (comprised of women and men). As time went on, some women became powerful politically in the convents and monasteries. They usually came from the upper classes and were better educated than the peasants. Unfortunately, their skills and abilities were not always put to use for the good of the community or the church, as were the abilities of men.

With the coming of the Reformation in the 16th century, many things changed. However, the attitude toward women and their contribution to the church changed very slowly. The perspective of the Reformers toward marriage was very similar to that of the Catholic Church. The primary calling for women was as wives and mothers who were to be subordinate to men. In spite of this, some women with leadership gifts, powerful skills and devotion to God made important contributions to the church as it was undergoing reformation.

Many of them had been Catholic nuns who had been educated in convents — about the only place where women were permitted education in the Middle Ages. Perhaps the most well known is Teresa of Avila, writer, a mystic and church reformer.

Some women of noble birth became influential in the Reformation. Among them were Marguerite of Navarre and her daughter, Jeanne d'Albert, who, after her conversion became a powerful supporter of the French Huguenots. There were many other courageous women reformers, some of whom were burned at the stake or suffered other horrendous tortures for their faith.

In the New World, prejudice was strong against women leaders, although they kept appearing despite great efforts to limit their work anywhere except in the home. For example, Anne Hutchinson was the most well known of the women preachers of colonial times, despite great opposition to her leadership. Women evangelists become more common during the great revivals. They often held revival meetings, but were rarely pastors in the 18th and 19th centuries. They met the same kinds of resistance to their ministries that is found today. Perhaps the most well-known woman evangelist was Phoebe Palmer, who became known as "the mother of the Holiness Movement."

The women's missionary movement of the 19th century was the result of the failure of most denominational mission boards to appoint single women to the kind of work that used their full gifts and callings. Because of this, many women's boards were developed which appointed only single women. Their work grew rapidly and was enormously successful. Soon there were thousands of single women missionaries serving around the world. By 1890, India alone had more than 700 single women missionaries.

Beginning in the early 20th century, most denominational boards were appointing single women for a variety of ministries. They appealed for the women's boards to combine with them. Eventually, all of the women's missionary boards were taken over by the general denominational mission boards.

Today, there are many more women missionaries than men. Single male missionaries are rare, but there are many single women missionaries serving in much the same kinds of work as men. They preach, translate the Bible, plant churches, begin and administer schools, hospitals, and Bible schools.

Where does that leave the church today? We all recognize that many Christians believe that the ministry of women should be largely limited to the home, or to work with children, or to work with other women. Yet, nearly all churches around the world include many more women than men. Is evangelism advanced when we place limitations on women carrying the message of Christ? Are the churches advancing the great commission when they limit women's service? This is where we

17

must consider the theological, cultural and social challenges facing the work of God in the world.

In this Occasional Paper, we offer the perspective of Christian scholars and lay leaders from many countries, every continent, representing many denominations as they face these crucial questions and their responsibilities in spreading the gospel of Christ.

The question of women being empowered along with men to minister to the whole church is an issue of church governance and an assessment of the Biblical stance. It is not an issue which reduces in any way the gospel message and those who take one view or another cannot be criticised on the grounds that Biblical authority has been ignored. Rather, it is a matter of interpretation of the passages that leads us in different directions. Both those who take the position that women should not be in a leadership role and those who grant women leadership respect the authority of the Scriptures and yet both groups advance the gospel message with great passion and devotion.

In the last few decades, the issue of abuse — sexual, physical, emotional, spiritual — has come into the spotlight in many parts of the world. Different cultures respond differently. We see how abuse weakens evangelism and what the church can do to address it.

Through the writings and experiences of people from many cultures, we observe how the issue of gender confronts the cultures and branches of the church around the world, and how Christian leaders are dealing with gender barriers that weaken the gospel message. Although gender issues have been with us since the beginning of the world, only recently have Christians begun to deal honestly with all of their ramifications and their effects on the spread of the gospel.

C. Historical Models of Women Leaders in the Church
by Mimi Haddad

Since the time of Jesus, women have worked beside men on the frontiers of evangelism and missions. Women, like men, preached the gospel, translated the Bible, planted churches, built denominations and institutions and died as martyrs. They counted the approval of the world as nothing, compared with the privilege of serving Christ. Yet, their names are often unfamiliar to Christians today.

Excluding the last 25 years, history has largely ignored women. Only recently have historians uncovered the past of marginalized groups such as women. Here we will explore examples of women, from the early church to the modern era, who used their gifts to advance Christ's kingdom.

Thecla (First Century)
A renowned missionary of the early church was Thecla, a young woman from a wealthy family. Thecla heard Paul preach and despite the disapproval of her family, she became a Christian who abandoned the comfort of her class. She served Christ as an ascetic and missionary near Antioch, where she had a dynamic ministry of preaching, teaching and healing. Thecla's legacy is remembered by two early church fathers, who spoke of Thecla's ministry in Syria as a centre of teaching and healing. A team of German archaeologists excavated her hospital in 1908, describing its dimensions as the size of a football field.

Apollonia of Alexandria (249 AD)
Apollonia was martyred in Alexandria, Egypt, under the Roman emperor Decius. She had served the church for many years as a deacon. In 249 an angry mob gathered a group of Christians, including the elderly woman Appolonia. They knocked out her teeth, and built a fire on which she was to burn to death unless she renounced her faith in Christ. Asking for a moment to consider their proposition, she gave her pursuers a chance to back away from her, after which she lunged into the flames, ending her life. After her death, a church was erected in her honour in Rome.

Paula who worked with Jerome (347 - 404 AD)
These two prepared one of the earliest translations of the Bible. Paula was a wealthy Roman woman who became a devout Christian after the death of her husband. She gave away her vast fortune to build hospitals and care for the poor. Paula mastered the Hebrew language, and her linguistic skills were a priceless resource to Jerome as they translated the Bible from Hebrew and Greek into Latin, the common language of that day.

In gratitude for Paula's assistance, Jerome dedicated some of his work to her. He wrote, "*There are people, O Paula, who take offence at seeing your name at the beginning of my works. These people do not know that while Barak trembled, Deborah saved Israel; that Esther delivered from supreme peril the children of God . . . Is it not to women that our Lord appeared after His resurrection? Yes, and the men could then blush for not having sought what women had found.*"

Hildegard of Bingen (1098 – 1179)

Hildegard was a physician, a composer of music, a poet and she was deeply involved in the politics of her day. She laboured tirelessly to revive the spiritual health of a church that had become indifferent. A Benedictine nun and abbess over a double monastery, she urged people to look to the Bible and to Christ rather than to the priests. A great mystic, her writings were collected in the book, "Know the Ways of the Lord."

Elizabeth of Hungary (1207 – 1231)

She fed starving people, built hospitals for lepers, and was known to remove her jewels before entering the chapel, foreshadowing the day when she would give away her vast wealth on behalf of the poor.

Her husband shared her faith and her commitment to good works. As famine ravaged their land, Elizabeth ordered the royal bakers and cooks to work through the night preparing bread and soup to feed the poor. Nuns and monks worked alongside Elizabeth distributing food to some 900 hungry people. As the famine persisted, Elizabeth opened soup kitchens throughout the land and urged that churches be made available for the homeless. She eventually emptied her own pantry to care for the poor, and sold her jewels and precious metals to meet the needs of the people.

Catherine of Sienna (1347 – 1380)

Corruption, violence, plague, and political and spiritual wickedness were unbridled during the life of this Italian, Dominican nun. When very young, Catherine had visions of Christ that led her into a life of spiritual discipline and material simplicity. At age 16, Catherine moved into a small room where she lived in solitude for three years.

At the age of 21, God called her to public service in Sienna. During the plague, she cared for the sick and dying. She ministered to those wrongly imprisoned. When a young man had been unjustly condemned, Catherine cared for the man and remained with him through his execution, stirring the conscience of the town. Her wisdom spread, and soon a group of disciples, from many parts of society shadowed her ministry.

Catherine was a mystic and throughout her life she experienced visions of God. She demanded that the spiritual rulers of her day mirror Christ. She believed God had called her to speak against the church leaders who were oppressing the people. She denounced the greed and spiritual poverty of the clergy.

She boldly confronted the Pope in Avignon and reminded him of the church's highest mission of saving souls. After she had delivered a message to the Pope, he turned to the cardinals and exclaimed, "Behold my brethren, how contemptible we are before God. . . This poor woman puts us to shame. . . It is she who encourages us."

Teresa of Avila (1515 – 1582)
This Spanish, Carmelite nun was Jewish by birth. Her grandparents had converted to Christianity during the Spanish inquisition. A writer, a mystic, and a church reformer, she is perhaps the most celebrated woman in church history. She once fell into a trance and had a vision in which she believed God was calling her to a life of prayer.

In her book, *The Interior Castle,* she illustrated through analogy the soul's journey toward intimacy with God. Her work remains a classic in Christian spirituality.

She fought the greed and corruption within in her order. She began her reformation by calling the Carmelites back to their roots of simplicity. She established 16 convents built on her reform concepts. She was never free from persecution by the Carmelites who opposed her reforms. Teresa was aware of her constant peril. Her disciple, John of the Cross, advanced her reforms after her death.

THE REFORMATION AND MODERN MISSIONARY ERA
From the 1500's through the 1800's, women were prominent martyrs, reformers and missionaries.

Anne Askew (1521 – 1546)

A Protestant reformer during the English Reformation, she was imprisoned, tortured and finally burned at the stake for her faith. When questioned about her faith, she calmly defended her right to read, study and argue her interpretations of Scripture. Born into a wealthy family, she was highly educated and keenly interested in theology. She challenged male authority and out-reasoned her interrogators, using their own logic against them.

Catherine Booth (1829 – 1890)

She was co-founder, with her husband William Booth, of the Salvation Army. She was a powerful preacher and a tenacious inner city missionary.

Concerning the public ministry of women, Catherine was outraged when Phoebe Palmer's speaking tour in England was criticised because Palmer spoke to both men and women. Catherine therefore wrote a pamphlet, "Female Ministry, or Woman's Right to Preach the Gospel," a remarkable defence of women's biblical call to preach.

When her husband, William, became ill, Catherine assumed his circuit preaching duties. From its beginning, the Salvation Army has protected the ministry of women preaching and teaching.

Catherine was also involved in the temperance movement, inner city missions and work among prostitutes. She said, "It will be a happy day for England when Christian ladies transfer their attention from poodles to destitute and starving children."

Charlotte "Lottie" Moon (1840 – 1912)

Born to a wealthy Virginia plantation owner, her mother read to her children the life of Ann Adoniram Judson. This inspired Lottie to consider service as a missionary.

She received a Master's degree from Hollins College in 1851. Turning down an offer for marriage, she sailed for China in 1873. She quickly assimilated the Chinese language and culture and eventually settled in Pingtu, where no missionary had ventured. There she began a church, later a school and an orphanage, living in a Chinese house (unlike the usual "missionary compounds"), eating Chinese food and wearing Chinese clothes.

Moon persevered through serious famines, revolutions, and plagues. Money was always short and she appealed to her women friends at home for help. There was never enough, and she eventually died of malnutrition because she could not bear to eat with hungry Chinese children looking on. She shared everything she had. The "Southern Baptist Lottie Moon offering" now raises millions of dollars a year for missions.

Amy Carmichael (1868 – 1951)

She lived and worked more than fifty years in India, writing 35 books on missionary work. She devoted her life to serving Indian children, especially rescuing more than 2000 girls from a life of temple prostitution. Her work was dangerous, especially since the government of India endeavoured to keep the practice secret. At one point she had more than 900 girls and workers in her school.

Amanda Smith (1837 – 1915)

Born into slavery in the U.S., Amanda saw the influence of her mother and grandmother. Through their godly lives and prayers, her slave owner's daughter had come to faith. Later Amanda was deeply influenced by the second great religious awakening. In one such meeting, Amanda felt called of God to preach the gospel. Following the Civil War, she preached all over the US and in England, India, and Africa.

Like other women, she faced gender prejudice. Even her own denomination, the African Methodist Episcopal Church forbade the ordination of women. Opposition also came from white Christians. In England she met white Christians who were more concerned that a woman might preach than that people come to faith in Christ.

However, one male missionary in India where she preached wrote her: "I learned many valuable lessons from you more that have been of actual value to me as a preacher of Christian truth, than from any other person I have met."

Mary Slessor (1848 – 1915)

Mary was a Scottish factory worker who turned missionary and served in Calabar (present day Nigeria) for 38 years. She served in areas where few had dared to go.

Her only schooling was what she learned in her Scotch Presbyterian Sunday school. When she arrived in Africa at age 27, she was disillusioned by the rich life style of English missionaries. She moved in with Africans, ate their food, went without shoes, and finally moved to the bush were life was dangerous. Slessor adopted and raised several pairs of abandoned twins.

She won the respect of the Africans and she taught them the art of trade and their economy flourished. Slessor built schools, cared for the ill, preached and opened churches. As her African babies grew to adulthood, they began to take over her work and she moved further into the interior to begin again.

Pandita Ramabai (1858 - 1922)

Pandita founded the Mukti Mission in India that served needy women and children and was considered the best example of Christianity in action. Her father was a Brahmin priest married to a very young bride. When Pandita was 12, she had memorized 18,000 verses in Sanskrit and knew many other languages and dialects.

Both parents died when she and her brother were young. They wandered the countryside, homeless and hungry. She found and attended revival meetings where she learned of Christ's love for everyone, regardless of caste or gender. When she arrived in Calcutta, some educated men recognized her eloquence and learning. She became an example of the intellectual capacities of women. Eventually she made her way to America where she wrote her famous book "The High Caste Hindu Woman," that exposed the plight of women in India, including child brides, prostitution and lack of education. One crowd who heard her speak in Boston helped form the Ramabai Foundation, to support the work of educating India's child widows.

When Pandita died, hundreds attended her funeral, from many different castes, a testimony to a Christian woman who shaped the course of India's history.

Frances Willard (1839 - 1898)

A convert of Methodist revival meetings, Frances went on to become president of Women's Christian Temperance Union, one of the most influential organizations of the 19th century. She was an outspoken advocate of women's right to vote; she combated prostitution, exposed the need for laws against rape, and called fashion designers to eliminate pencil thin waistlines that deformed women's bodies.

Dwight L. Moody invited Willard to speak during his campaign in Boston. She was an advocate for women in ministry, encouraging women to not limit themselves to work among other women. She wrote to Mrs. Dwight L. Moody, *"I believe 'Women's Meetings' as such are a relic of an outworn regime. As in the day of Pentecost, so now, let men and women in perfectly impartial fashion participate in all services conducted in His name in whom there is neither bond nor free, male nor female, but all are one."*

Sojourner Truth (1797 – 1887)

Sojourner was a leading suffragist, preacher and social reformer. A slave named Isabella at birth, she remembered hearing her mother cry long into the night at the loss of her children who had been sold from their family. But her mother told the remaining children, *"Oh my children, there is a God who hears and sees you. Ask Him to help because He always hears you."*

Isabella was sold away from her parents at age 17. After giving birth to five children, she ran away, convinced that God affirmed freedom for slaves. She became a housekeeper for a Quaker couple and decided to change her name from Isabella to Sojourner Truth. She explained,

> *"My name was Isabella, but when I left the house of bondage, I left everything behind. I wasn't goin' to keep nothing' of Egypt on me, so I asked the Lord for a new name. And the Lord gave me Sojourner, because I was to travel up and down the land, showin' the people their sins. Afterward I told the Lord I wanted another name, 'cause everybody else had two names, and the Lord gave me Truth because I was to declare the truth to the people."*

Truth travelled from Connecticut to Massachusetts preaching as she went. So fiery were her sermons that the farmers would lay aside their work to hear her.

Abolitionists Frederick Douglas and William Lloyd Garrison persuaded her to speak on behalf of the American Antislavery Society.

Abolitionist lectures were often violent, but Truth was known for her fearlessness. Asked why, she said, *"I feel safe even in the midst of my enemies, for the truth is powerful and will prevail."*

When Sojourner rose to speak, her stature was so imposing, her voice was so powerful that none dared interrupt. During a suffragist convention in Ohio, Truth gave what was perhaps her most famous lecture on women's rights: *"I born my children and seen most of them sold to slavery, and when I cried out with a mother's grief, none but Jesus heard — and aren't I a woman? Den dat little man in black dar, he say women can't have as much rights as a man, cause Christ weren't a woman. Where did your Christ come from?"*

As she stood there with outstretched arms and eyes of fire, raising her voice still louder, she repeated, *"Where did your Christ come from? From God and a woman. Man had nothing to do with him."*

When Truth died in 1887, her funeral procession was attended by a thousand persons: abolitionists, suffragists and friends who recalled how Truth had reformed her country and had said how happy she was *"that the stars and stripes of the American flag no longer represent the scars and stripes of the slave."*

Conclusion:
We celebrate the lives of these women evangelists, leaders, bible translators and missionaries, thanking God for their legacy of leadership and service to Christ. Although church culture did not always receive these women with open arms, God gave them opportunity to use their God-given gifts in advancing Christ's kingdom. They brought the good news through word and deed, and in doing so, they left a legacy for us all.

2. The Biblical Basis for Women's Gospel Service

A. Paul and Women
by Mimi Haddad

Throughout history, women have been denied teaching and leadership roles based primarily on certain interpretations of the teachings of Paul. Even today there are thousands of churches that continue to suggest that Scripture prohibits women from leadership and preaching roles, often based on a certain interpretation of three passages written by the apostle Paul. What are the three verses? 1 Corinthians 14:34; 1 Timothy 2:11-15 and Ephesians 5: 22.

Why did Paul write these verses and how should we understand them today? To understand any passage in the Bible we must first ask what the passage meant to those to whom the letter was first written. What did it mean to the author? We ask this before we ask what it should mean to us.

Let's take a closer look at the Apostle Paul.

Paul was a great Bible scholar, a Jew among Jews and a strict Pharisee. He vigorously persecuted Christians before his conversion to Christ. Paul's training as a Pharisee held a very restrictive view of women. According to the Pharisees, women could not learn the Torah; they were silenced and excluded from priestly roles.

Yet Paul learned how women were prophesying at Pentecost. Pentecost was the birthday of the church when 3,000 came to faith from many tribes and nations (Acts 2:9-11). Pentecost also fulfilled Joel's prophecy that the Holy Spirit would gift all Christians for service, without regard to race, class or gender (Acts 2:17-18).

After his miraculous conversion, Paul became one of the greatest evangelists and leaders of the Christian faith. Despite the narrow requirements of the Jewish priesthood (first born, of a specific lineage, a male without blemish, etc.), Paul advanced the gifts of all believers — as a birthright of all those born of the Spirit. (See Acts 2 & 1 Corinthians 12). It was Paul who wrote Galatians 3:28: *There is neither Jew nor Greek, slave nor free, male nor female, for you are all one in Christ Jesus.* Galatians 3:28 is said, by the world's finest New Testament scholar — F.F. Bruce, to be the eye of the New Testament. Moreover,

27

Paul worked beside and empowered women who were leading house churches in cities like Ephesus and Philippi and Paul refers to them as his co-workers.

Because we believe the Bible does not contradict itself, we need to look closely at the women beside whom Paul laboured in the gospel. We must also understand the entire body of Paul's work when considering his comments regarding women in 1Corinthians 14:34, 1Timothy 2:11-15, and Ephesians 5: 22. Let us first consider the women who worked beside Paul.

Lydia in Acts 16:13-14, 40

This is the story of the first church in Europe. Paul encountered a group of women praying. Here Paul met Lydia, a wealthy merchant of purple and a woman of faith. The Lord opened her heart and her entire household was baptized. Her home became a house church, and the Scriptures suggest she was the leader of this church. In Paul's letter to the Philippians, he affirms his love for this church, the only church that regularly contributed to Paul's support and from which Paul accepted support. Philippians is one of Paul's most tender and personal letters. In the fourth chapter, Paul mentions two women from this church who were also his co-workers in the gospel, Euodia and Syntyche. These women "struggled beside" Paul in the work of the gospel. Paul affirms them as co-labourers in building the church.

Lydia was not the only woman leader of a house church. There was also the "elect lady," mentioned in 2 John 1:1, 13.

Priscilla and Aquila:

Paul mentions this couple more often than anyone else except Timothy. Priscilla and Aquila are an example of Galatians 3:28. Priscilla was a free, Roman woman. Aquila was Jewish and a freed slave. When the Jews were banished from Rome by decree of Claudius, Priscilla and Aquila left Italy, reaching Corinth before Paul, in 51 AD. After Paul arrived in Corinth, he lived with Priscilla and Aquila because they were tentmakers. Eighteen months later, all three relocated to Ephesus.

In Ephesus, Priscilla and Aquila gained prominence, not only through the church they established in their home (1 Corinthians 16:19), but also by risking their lives for Paul (perhaps during the riots mentioned in Acts19:23-41), a deed for which *all* the Gentile churches gave thanks (Romans 16:4).

Luke tells how Priscilla and Aquila instructed Apollos — who although he was well versed in the Scripture, he lacked some theological insights, which Priscilla and Aquila provided. Apollos received Priscilla's instruction without reservation. Far from condemning her for having taught a man, both Luke and Paul acknowledge Priscilla.

Priscilla's authority in the early church is highlighted by Paul, who calls her his "co-worker" (Romans 16:3), a term Paul uses to identify leaders such as Mark, Timothy, Titus, Philemon and Luke. Moreover, her name is mentioned first in four of the six references to Priscilla and Aquila, suggesting she was the more distinguished of the two. Both Luke and Paul honour her in this way.

If Paul intended Priscilla to be silent, she could not have taught Apollos, nor planted churches in Corinth, Ephesus or Rome without his censure.

Phoebe Romans 16:1.
Paul calls her a deacon [*diakonos*] — a term used 21 times in the New Testament. When used of male leaders in the church, it is translated "minister" by the King James Version, but when used of Phoebe it is translated "servant."

Phoebe was a *diakonos* in the church in Cenchrea. Commentators suggest she carried Paul's letters between Rome and Greece, a hazardous stretch across rough waters and 100 miles of rocky terrain. Phoebe had to be strong of heart, spirit and body and Paul had to trust her.

Paul also refers to Phoebe as his *prostatis,* or benefactor. Literally this means one who is in authority or one who presides. (Thayer's Greek-English Lexicon) This is the only place in the New Testament where this noun appears. Paul uses the verb form of *prostates* in 1 Thessalonians 5:12 where it means exercising leadership.

Eunice and Lois
These two women were the mother and grandmother of Paul's closest co-worker, Timothy. In 2 Timothy 1:5 Paul wrote: "*I am*

reminded of your sincere faith, a faith that lived first in your grandmother Lois and your mother Eunice and now, I am sure lives in you." He goes on to add, "*But as for you, continue in what you have learned and firmly believed, knowing from whom you learned it, and how from infancy you have known the Holy Scriptures which are able to make you wise for salvation through faith in Christ.*" (2 Timothy 3:14-15). Lois and Eunice were far from silent, but instructed Paul's closest disciple.

Examining Paul's relationships demonstrates his partnership with women in a wide variety of ministry and leadership contexts. Consistent with this, Paul's teaching on the spiritual gifts gives further witness that the spiritual gifts are not designated according to gender. If Paul intended women to be silent, why did he not indicate this in his instructions on spiritual gifts, in 1Corinthians 12:7ff, Romans 12:6-8 and Ephesians 4:11? In these three letters, Paul states that spiritual gifts are to be used to build up and edify the church. Yet, he never suggests that the gifts are given along gender lines. These gifts include evangelists, prophets, pastors, teachers and apostles. Furthermore, we can identify New Testament women who had these gifts and served the church, alongside Paul, as evangelists, prophets, teachers and apostles. In fact, Paul identifies a woman apostle in Rom 16, namely, Junia. She was not only an apostle, but exemplary among the apostles.

Given Paul's work beside women leaders in the early church, coupled with his comments on the spiritual gifts, why do we have these three oft-quoted passages that seem to prohibit women's leadership? Do these three passages nullify Paul's clear affirmation of women's authority to speak and teach in the church? Is Paul limiting women at all times, or is he calling for specific women in specific churches to be limited due to a local problem?

Our challenge is to understand the situation in those churches. Let's look at each passage.

1 Corinthians 14:34-36

> *As in all the churches of the saints, women should be silent in the churches. For they are not permitted to speak but should be subordinate, as the law also says. If there is anything they desire to know, let them ask their husbands at home. For it is shameful for a woman to speak in church. Or did the word of God*

originate with you? Or are you the only ones it has reached?

Paul's letter to the church in Corinth reveals a troubled church. Corinth was one of the richest, most decadent cities in the ancient world. In it was the temple of the goddess Aphrodite — a temple that boasted of 1,000 prostitutes. Writing from Ephesus, Paul had learned of specific problems, which his letter addressed. What was the trouble in Corinth?

- Divided loyalties. Some claimed to belong to Paul, some to Peter, some to Apollos and some to Christ.
- Sexual immorality within the Church. Corinth was a centre for sex, with temple prostitutes who served at the infamous temple of Aphrodite.
- Eating food sacrificed to idols.
- Disorderly worship.
- How women should dress when praying or prophesy in church. Paul seems equally concerned with men's apparel. Men, Paul claims, should pray with their heads uncovered.

Paul asks women to be silent in the church in Corinth (1Corinthians 14:34). This must be viewed in light of his comments, three chapters earlier, when he tells women how to dress when speaking, *"But any woman who prays and prophesies with her head unveiled disgraces her head"* (1Corinthians 11:5 NIV). Paul is instructing women how to dress when praying and prophesying. It is hard to prophesy while being silent. Clearly, Paul's instruction to silence women appears at the end of his exhortation to teach the gospel in an orderly way, so others might understand the gospel (1Corinthians 14:1-36). It is probable that women were speaking in a manner that Paul considered disorderly and inappropriate (perhaps similar to the way women worshipped in the Greek cults) and thus Paul asks them to cover their heads. Because these (married) women are proving disruptive, Paul instructs them to bring their questions to their husbands at home so that their concerns might be addressed. Paul's priority, however, is for orderly teaching, that women's questions not disrupt the learning of others. This passage works to address a specific problem in Corinth and should not be viewed as universal in application.

1 Timothy 2:11-15

Let a woman learn in silence with full submission. I permit no woman to teach or to have authority over a

31

man; she is to keep silent. For Adam was formed first, then Eve, and Adam was not deceived, but the woman was deceived and became a transgressor. Yet she will be saved through childbearing, provided they continue in faith and love and holiness, with modesty.

I Tim 2:11-15 is perhaps the most frequently quoted passage used to prohibit women from using their leadership and teaching gifts. Paul raises three significant issues in the above passage, which may be summarized by three questions. (1) Does Paul suggest that women shall never exercise authority or to speak in the Church? (2) What is the significance of Eve in the above passage? (3) Why would Paul argue that women are saved by childbirth? We shall answer each question in turn. But first, let us consider the historical background of Paul's letter to Timothy.

Paul's personal letter to Timothy (not addressed to the church) is a tender message from Paul, written to his loyal and trusted co-worker. Paul wishes to help Timothy encourage a troubled church in Ephesus, which, like Corinth, was a centre of debauchery. The temple of Artemis was considered one of the seven wonders of the Ancient world. Artemis was a fertility goddess who had many worshippers throughout Asia, especially in Ephesus. (Acts 19:24, 27-28, 34-35) She was said to protect women in childbirth. According to legend, Artemis attended the birth of Alexander the Great.

The basic thrust of 1 Timothy is a treatise against false teaching in the church at Ephesus. The first chapter defines the faulty teachings, which Paul calls myths and endless genealogies, whereby some have shipwrecked their faith (1 Timothy 1:3-7, 19-20). False teachers, perhaps some of whom were women, were clearly troubling the church at Ephesus.

In the context of false teaching, we observe Paul's call for women's silence in the church. Would Timothy have understood Paul as silencing all women for all time? Hardly. Timothy was aware of the success Priscilla and Aquila had in instructing Apollos in Ephesus and also in building house churches. Paul's last letter to Timothy, just before his execution in Rome, instructs Timothy to greet Priscilla and Aquila, as they had apparently returned to Ephesus to help Timothy (2 Timothy 4:19). Paul would not have instructed Timothy to receive help from Priscilla and Aquila if he believed she was out of order. Nor would Paul ask Timothy to involve Priscilla in a teaching, mentoring or leadership position if he believed this to be an unbiblical position for a woman. Rather, it is Paul's implied commendation of her ministry of leadership.

It is important to note that Paul prefaces his silence of women in Ephesus with a call for women to learn. Possibly the women were advancing myths regarding Artemis. Clearly, they were unschooled in the truths of their own faith. To suggest that women should learn was radical! Rabbis were said to learn in silence. This would hardly be Paul's approach if the goal was to ensure their continued silence in public meetings.

Moreover, Paul utilizes a word that is commonly translated "authority" in the same sentence. The word "authority" in verse 12, which in Greek is *authentein*, appears only this once in the Bible. The usual word for authority is *exousia*. In fact, *authentein* is very rare in other Greek literature as well. There are several possible meanings including "to usurp or to dominate." Some scholars say it can mean to behave in a violent way.

It is clear from Jesus' instructions to the disciples that those who exercise authority should never domineer,[i] so it is reasonable for Paul to forbid women to exercise authority in a way that would be a poor model for any believer. However, just as Jesus was not forbidding the exercise of authority in a godly manner, neither is Paul suggesting that women are not to exercise authority, but they are not to exercise *abusive* authority as suggested by this unusual verb.

Another dynamic of this passage is Paul's reference to Adam being formed first, before Eve. Being first does not indicate leadership or final authority. Remember, John the Baptist came before Christ and the insects were created before Adam and Eve. Yet, Paul seems to be drawing parallels between Eve, who was deceived and those who were teaching false doctrine in Ephesus. In Genesis 2:16-17, God gave Adam — who was formed first (not Eve) the prohibitions of Eden — which trees to eat from and which to avoid. Eve, like the women in Ephesus, learned God's commandments second-hand and Paul is asking them to learn. Once educated then they too might become skilled teachers like Priscilla, whom many in Ephesus probably knew.

---

[i] David Hamilton, Why Not Women? (YWAM Publishing, 2000), 223-4

Lastly, we should not under-estimate the influence of Artemis, who was widely worshipped in Ephesus. According to the myth, Artemis helped women, especially in childbirth. In confronting false teaching in Ephesus, Paul suggests that women will be saved through childbirth. Is Paul implying that women will be saved in childbirth not through the worship of Artemis, but by remaining faithful to Christ? After all, it was through woman (Mary) that Christ was born.[ii] It is unlikely that Paul would create one system of salvation for men — salvation through faith in Christ, and another for women — childbirth. Therefore, we conclude that women were involved in false teaching, perhaps by incorporating not only the teachings of Artemis but also by exercising abusive authority and Paul asks them to study their faith more carefully.

Ephesians 5:21-22

Be subject to one another out of reverence for Christ. Wives, be subject to your husbands as to the Lord. For the husband is the head (kephale) of the wife just as Christ is the head (kephale) of the church, the body of which he is the Savior. Just as the church is subject to Christ, so also wives ought to be, in everything to their husbands.

Many Bibles (including the TNIV) begin the paragraph with verse 21 where the thought really begins. This passage, in the Greek Bible reads: *Submit yourselves to one another in deference to Christ. Wives to your husbands as to the Lord.*

Verse 22 lacks a verb. Translators place the verb from verse 21, into verse 22, which is proper. By beginning the paragraph in verse 21, we see the essence of Paul's thought. Paul says that all Christians should submit to each other and wives should submit themselves to their husbands. Does that mean a husband should also submit to his wife? Yes! This is the clear teaching of verse 21. Christians are to be known by their mutual submission. In verse 22, Paul adds a request for wives to submit. He is not removing his call for husbands to submit. Somehow, in many churches, women alone are called to submission. This does not adequately represent the biblical text. Remember the verb is submit, *not* obey. Submission is the call for voluntary deference.

[ii] Linda Belleville, The IVP Women's Bible Commentary (Downers Grove, IL: InterVarsity Press), 741.

This chapter goes on to say that Christ is head of the church, as the husband is head of the wife. Does that mean that he is the boss or authority? No. The word for boss or authority in Greek is typically *arcon*, not *kephale* — which is the noun used here. *Kephale* is best translated source, beginning or origin.

Paul also uses the word *kephale*, as head, in 1 Corinthians 11:3... "*I want you to understand that Christ is the head (kephale) of every man, and the husband is the head (kephale) of his wife, and God is the head (kephale) of Christ.*" Is Paul talking about authority here? No, *kephale* means source or origin.

In Ephesians 5:28 Paul refers back to the one-flesh relationship of Adam and Eve, described in Genesis 2. "*In the same way, husbands should love their wives as they do their own bodies. He who loves his wife loves himself. For no one ever hates his own body, but he nourishes and tenderly cares for it, just as Christ does for the church, because we are members of his body. For this reason a man will leave his father and mother and be joined to his wife and the two will become one flesh. This is a great mystery, and I am applying it to Christ and the church. Each of you, however, should love his wife as himself, and a wife should respect her husband.*"

In Genesis, God creates woman from the man's body. Likewise, Christ is the origin or source of the church. Christ died to bring others to life. In the same way, husbands are to love their wives sacrificially — as their own flesh. This underscores the idea of oneness, of intimacy.

The one-flesh relationship is an image of intimate communion, of mutuality and sacrificial love which prompts us to submit to one another, as noted in Ephesians 5:21. All Christians are to be characterized by their mutual submissiveness, for that is how the Church and marriage work best. It is the same intimacy and mutuality that operates within the God-head, between members of the Trinity. (1 Corinthians 11:3)

Christians are to submit themselves to one another (Ephesians 5:21). Wives are to submit to their husbands as their head and husbands are to love their wives as they love their own bodies. The language is not a military type of authority, but the language of love and intimacy, of the one-flesh relationship. So, Ephesians 5:21ff is not intended to place wives in a position subordinate to their husbands. Ephesians 5 seeks to build Christian marriages upon the foundation of love, unity, and oneness.

The only place where Paul talks exclusively about marriage is 1 Corinthians 7, where Paul gives the same instructions to husbands and wives regarding sex and the responsibility for maintaining the marriage. If Paul had intended that husbands rule their wives, we would expect to find some indication in this text on marriage. What we find, however, is complete mutuality.

If we are to read the Bible with understanding we must read it consistently, through the main stream of Paul's thought, which is most clearly articulated for us in Galatians 3:28.

The main thrust of Paul's teaching was that women are equally gifted by God and equally called to service in building the church, according to their spiritual gifts. Paul prohibits the public ministry of specific women in Corinth and Ephesus because they were exercising abusive authority and teaching false doctrine in Ephesus, and because of their disruptive behaviour in Corinth. However, Paul makes it clear that women should learn correct theology (1Timothy 2:11), so that their behaviour might be consistent with correct doctrine. Finally, Paul calls all Christians to submit to one another, in Ephesians 5:21. He also asks husbands to love their wives sacrificially, just as Christ loved the church. To ask first century husbands to love their wives, and to love them as they love their own body was most radical indeed.

B. A Map for Gender Reconciliation
by Jane Crane

It is clear from in-depth study of the relevant Scriptures, including those that appear to limit women in ministry, that Scripture is far more favourable to women in ministry than has previously been thought. To understand the meaning of the Scriptures, it is important to grasp their cultural context, the full grasp of the Greek words used and an overview of the Scriptures on women as a whole. Also of prime significance is the revolutionary way Jesus included women, especially in light of the culture and customs of his day.

While different scholars and denominations hold different positions, the groundbreaking research of the last two decades in particular has shed important light on the matter. It is now clear that the relevant Scriptures cannot be understood with just a surface reading. The following "Map for Gender Reconciliation" is a guideline for personal study to reconcile what the Scriptures say about women in ministry. The expanded Map for Gender Reconciliation (see box on Map), as well as the many books and articles listed in the "Suggested Reading" at the end of this occasional paper, provide a wealth of information for study.

Map for Gender Reconciliation™

"Therefore, if anyone is in Christ, there is a new creation: The old is gone, the new has come! All this is from God, who reconciled us to himself through Christ and gave us the ministry of reconciliation: that God was reconciling the world to himself in Christ, not counting people's sins against them. And he has committed to us the message of reconciliation" (2 Cor. 5:17-19).

YES Women in Ministry? **NO?**

Needs study to evaluate

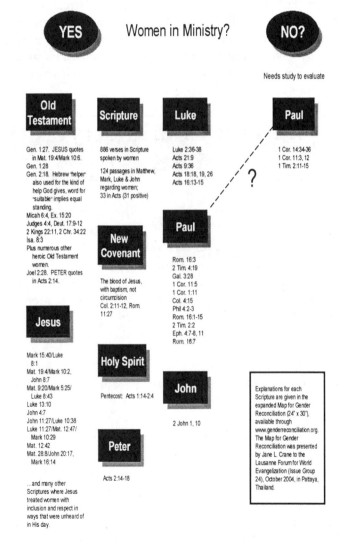

Old Testament

Gen. 1:27. JESUS quotes in Mat. 19:4/Mark 10:6.
Gen. 1:28
Gen. 2:18. Hebrew "helper" also used for the kind of help God gives, word for "suitable" implies equal standing.
Micah 6:4, Ex. 15:20
Judges 4:4, Deut. 17:9-12
2 Kings 22:11, 2 Chr. 34:22
Isa. 8:3
Plus numerous other heroic Old Testament women.
Joel 2:28. PETER quotes in Acts 2:14.

Scripture

886 verses in Scripture spoken by women

124 passages in Matthew, Mark, Luke & John regarding women; 33 in Acts (31 positive)

Luke

Luke 2:36-38
Acts 21:9
Acts 9:36
Acts 18:18, 19, 26
Acts 16:13-15

Paul

1 Cor. 14:34-36
1 Cor. 11:3, 12
1 Tim. 2:11-15

?

New Covenant

The blood of Jesus, with baptism, not circumcision
Col. 2:11-12, Rom. 11:27

Paul

Rom. 16:3
2 Tim. 4:19
Gal. 3:28
1 Cor. 11:5
1 Cor. 1:11
Col. 4:15
Phil 4:2-3
Rom. 16:1-15
2 Tim. 2:2
Eph. 4:7-8, 11
Rom. 16:7

Jesus

Mark 15:40/Luke 8:1
Mat. 19:4/Mark 10:2, John 8:7
Mat. 9:20/Mark 5:25/ Luke 8:43
Luke 13:10
John 4:7
John 11:27/Luke 10:38
Luke 11:27/Mat. 12:47/ Mark 10:29
Mat. 12:42
Mat. 28:8/John 20:17, Mark 16:14
...and many other Scriptures where Jesus treated women with inclusion and respect in ways that were unheard of in His day.

Holy Spirit

Pentecost: Acts 1:14-2:4

John

2 John 1, 10

Peter

Acts 2:14-18

Explanations for each Scripture are given in the expanded Map for Gender Reconciliation (24" x 30"), available through www.genderreconciliation.org. The Map for Gender Reconciliation was presented by Jane L. Crane to the Lausanne Forum for World Evangelization (Issue Group 24), October 2004, in Pattaya, Thailand.

Map for Gender Reconciliation™ Scripture Explanations

Traditionally men as a gender have been fully released in ministry, and often women have not. The following Scriptures on the subject are presented to both men and women for study and prayer. First are the Scriptures that appear to be favourable to women in ministry (the Yes's), followed by those that have been thought to limit women in ministry (the No's).

Women in Ministry?
YES

OLD TESTAMENT

Creation: God makes male and female "in His own image." Jesus quotes this in Matthew 19:4, Mark 10:6. God blesses "them," tells "them" to rule over every living creature. Words for creation of female imply equality, the kind of help God gives. Hebrew *'ezer k^eneged* (Genesis 1:26-28, 2:18).

Miriam: A leader in Israel. Micah 6:4 quotes God as saying that He sent Moses, also Aaron and Miriam, to lead the Israelites. She is also called a prophet (Exodus 15:20).

Deborah: The judge/leader of Israel in her time and a prophet. Judges 4:4 tells us that she was leading Israel (NIV). Deuteronomy 17:9-12 describes the authority that she as the judge of Israel had, saying that anyone showing contempt for a judge would be put to death.

Huldah: A prophet who was consulted by the high priest and other leaders when the king wanted a word from the Lord after the Book of the Law was found. She gave a strong word of prophecy (2 Kings 22:11-20; 2 Chronicles 34:22-28).

Isaiah's wife: Referred to as a prophet (Isaiah 8:3).

Women prophesying: The prophet Joel quotes God as saying that He will pour out His Spirit on all people.   Sons and daughters will prophesy. God will pour out His Spirit even on men and women servants (Joel 2:28-29).   Peter quotes this Scripture in the New Testament as being fulfilled on the day of Pentecost (Acts 2:16-18).

JESUS

Jesus' actions toward women have been called revolutionary for His culture.   When Jesus was born, the position of women had degraded greatly in the 400 years since Old Testament times.   The strong anti-women bias of the Greeks, who had invaded the Jews, had impacted Jewish thought and custom.   The leading Greeks philosophers had contempt for women.   In Jesus' day a Jewish woman was not allowed to speak in a synagogue, had to sit in a separate part of the synagogue from the men, was generally not allowed to study the Scriptures as a man could, and was even not to speak to a man in public other than her husband.   She was considered inferior to men and her worth was in her childbearing capability, especially for sons.   Like the Greek myth of Pandora, women were blamed for all man's troubles because of Eve's actions in the Garden of Eden. In a common prayer of the day prayed daily by Jewish men, they thanked God for not making them women. But Jesus was different.   He treated women with inclusion and respect in ways that were unheard of in His day…

Mark 15:40 & Luke 8:1-3

When Jewish women were generally supposed to stay at home and not even talk to most men in public, many women travelled with Jesus.   He allowed the women to support him financially, humbling himself to receive from them in a day when men were the ones in charge of the finances and women were considered by many to be a disgrace.

Mat. 19:4-9 & Mark 10:2-9, John 8:7

When asked about divorce by the religious leaders, Jesus brought them back to what the eminent theologian F. F. Bruce has called "first principles." [1]   Jesus said that at the beginning God created male and female, so a man should leave his father and mother and be united to his wife, with the two becoming one.   In so doing, Jesus went against the culture of His day that the woman was not a valuable equal, and that she was expected to leave her family to be married to her husband essentially

40

as a possession. Again, Jesus defended women when He would not condemn the woman taken in adultery. By saying that anyone there without sin should throw the first stone, Jesus came against the self-righteous attitude of those present, as well as the double standard where the man was not being held accountable for his sin. He also treated the woman as valuable when he told her to go and sin no more.

Mat. 9:20 & Mark 5:25 & Luke 8:43
When the woman with the issue of blood touched Jesus' hem and was healed, Jesus' response shattered three religious taboos of His day regarding women. First, a woman with an issue of blood was considered "unclean" by the Jews, and if she touched a man he had to go through purification rites, yet Jesus in no way responded as if she had made Him unclean. Second, a Jewish woman was not supposed to speak in public to a religious teacher, and vice versa, yet Jesus called her to public dialogue and responded in a loving manner to her, calling her "daughter." Third, Jesus affirmed her faith in front of the crowd in a time when women were considered so inferior that it was said to be shameful for them to read aloud publicly from the Jewish religious teachings.

Luke 13:10-17
Jesus called a crippled woman forward into a synagogue where women were not allowed, only men, and healed her body. He even called her a "daughter of Abraham" when women were considered inferior and never called that; only men were called "sons of Abraham." Thus Jesus included women in spiritual life equally in two profound, and unheard of, ways.

John 4:7-26
In a day when Jewish men were not supposed to talk to women in public other than their wives, Jesus' longest recorded conversation in the Bible with any individual was in a public setting with a woman, the Samaritan woman at the well. He patiently answered all her questions, when women were not accorded such opportunity, and it was to this woman that Jesus revealed the great revelation that God is Spirit and his worshipers must worship in Spirit and truth. Jesus told this woman that He was the Messiah. She then told her village about Jesus and many believed in Him because of her testimony.

41

John 11:27, Luke 10:38

In a day when women were generally considered inferior and not worthy or capable of studying the Scriptures, two people in the Gospels are reported to have had a revelation that Jesus was Messiah, one of whom was a woman, Martha (the other was Peter). Also, in Jesus' day, the phrase to "sit at one's feet" meant to be a student learning from a teacher. Therefore, when Mary sat at Jesus' feet, she was his student, an amazing thing in His time. Further, Jesus rebuked Martha when she tried to call Mary away to work, saying Mary had chosen the better part.

Luke 11:27, Matthew 12:47, Mark 10:29

When a woman cried out that Jesus' mother was blessed for giving him birth and nursing him, Jesus refuted her. He set a broader standard for women when he said that blessed rather are those who hear the word of God and obey it. Jesus later repeated this theme when he said that whoever did the will of His Father in heaven was His brother and sister and mother, specifically adding the word *sister* when the original statement to him mentioned only his mother and brothers. He again included women twice when he said that no one who has left home or brothers or sisters or mother or father or children or fields for Him will fail to receive 100 times as much.

Matthew 12:42

In Jesus' culture women were considered so inferior that they could not even give testimony in a court and were considered inferior to a man with no say or authority over them. Yet Jesus said that a woman, the Queen of Sheba, would rise in judgment and condemn the generation of His day.

Matthew 28:8-10 & John 20:17, Mark 16:14

In Jesus' day when it was considered disgraceful for women to even read the Scriptures aloud, and their testimony was considered so unreliable that it would not be accepted in a court of law, Jesus appeared first after His resurrection to some women and gave them the first commission to report that He was resurrected. Jesus later rebuked the disciples for not believing their reports.

...and many other Scriptures where Jesus acknowledged and included women in ways that were extraordinary for His culture.

SCRIPTURE

886 verses in Scripture by women. [2] *124 passages in Matthew, Mark, Luke and John regarding women, 33 in Acts.*

In a day when women did not often appear in literature, and especially in a positive light, numerous Scriptures in the Gospels and Acts describe women.

NEW COVENANT

Colossians 2:11-12

In the new covenant through the blood of Jesus, the mark of the believer changes from a gender-exclusive one, circumcision, to a gender-inclusive one, baptism.

HOLY SPIRIT

Acts 1:14-2:4

On Pentecost, after 120 men and women had been praying continuously, all of them were filled with the Holy Spirit and began to speak in languages they did not know, declaring the glories of God to visitors in Jerusalem for the holy day.

PETER

Acts 2:14-18

On the great day of Pentecost, when the 120 men and women were filled with the Holy Spirit and speaking in foreign languages they did not know, Peter spoke to the amazed crowd and said that what was happening was prophesied by the Old Testament prophet Joel, specifically including women. Peter restated that sons and daughters will prophesy and that God will pour out His Spirit even on his servants, both men and women.

LUKE

33 references to women in the book of Acts

In a day when it was rare to even mention women in literature, and Jews generally excluded women from religious study and any significant participation, Luke refers to women 33 times in his writing of the book of Acts. He said they too believed and were baptized. He tells us three different times that both men and women were being persecuted and put in prison for their faith (Acts 8:3, 9:1-2, 22:4)..

Luke 2:36-38

In his Gospel, Luke tells us that when Mary and Joseph were presenting the baby Jesus to the Lord at the temple, the prophet Anna gave thanks to God and spoke of the child all were looking forward to as the redemption of Israel.

Acts 21:9

Luke states in the book of Acts that the evangelist Philip had four unmarried daughters who prophesied.

Acts 9:36

Luke describes a disciple named Tabitha, or "Dorcas" in the Greek, who was always doing good and helping the poor. She must have been greatly admired, because when she died of an illness the disciples urged Peter, who was in a town nearby, to come at once. He then raised her from the dead, and as a result many people believed in the Lord.

Acts 18:18, 19, 26

In a day when it was very rare to list a woman's name before a man's in referring to a couple, if her name were mentioned at all, Luke placed Priscilla's name first several times. This was a strong indication that Priscilla was the more respected of the two, as confirmed by the fourth-century bishop in Constantinople, Chrysostom. [3] Luke even placed Priscilla's name first (as seen in the original Greek) when Priscilla and Aquila explained the way of God more fully, to the great teacher Apollos.

Acts 16:13-15

Luke tells that Paul had a vision where he was called to Macedonia. There at a place of prayer by the river with a group of women, the first recorded convert to Christianity in all of Europe was a woman named Lydia, a dealer of purple cloth. Scripture tells us that the Lord opened her heart to respond to Paul's message, and that she and the members of her household were baptized.

Romans 16:3, 2 Tim. 4:19

Like Luke, Paul referred to Priscilla's name before her husband's two times, which was nearly unheard of in his culture. He greeted them, with her name first, in his letter to the Romans and called them his co-workers. He again greeted them in the same order in his second letter to Timothy. Paul had travelled with them (Acts 18:18), so he certainly knew them well.

Galatians 3:28

Paul makes the sweeping statement regarding gender equality, which was revolutionary, especially for his day, that for all those who are clothed with Christ, "There is neither Jew nor Greek, neither slave nor free, neither male nor female, for you are all one in Christ Jesus."

1 Corinthians 11:5

Paul describes head coverings for women who pray or prophesy.

1 Corinthians 1:11, Colossians 4:15

Paul cites reports from Chloe's household. He also sends greetings to Nympha and "the church in her house." Paul uses the same phrases regarding Chloe and Nympha that he does to describe the house churches of Aristobulus, Narcissus, Stephanas, Onesiphorus, and Priscilla and Aquila.

Philippians 4:2-3, Romans 16:1-15

In Philippians 4:2-3 Paul says that two women, Euodia and Syntyche, "*contended at his side*" in the cause of the gospel, along with the rest of his co-workers. Paul greets 29 co-workers in Romans 16:1-15, 10 of whom were women, and affirms their service to the Lord. He commends Phoebe to the Christians in Rome in glowing terms. He calls her a "deacon/minister" of the church (some translations say "servant" but the original Greek word used was *diakonos,* translated deacon/minister elsewhere in the New Testament). He uses the word *prostatis*, the only time it is used in the New Testament, to describe the kind of help she gave. This word describes patrons, those who had great impact and were highly esteemed.

2 Timothy 2:2, Ephesians 4:7-8, 11

In his second letter to Timothy, Paul says to entrust his teachings to reliable people who will be qualified to teach. The Greek word for "people" is *anthropos,* which means men and women, not *andros,* which means men only, and which Paul as a brilliant and precise writer could easily have chosen. In his letter to the Ephesians Paul uses the same word *anthropos* for both men and women when he says that Jesus ascended on high and gave gifts to his people. Paul then follows in verse 11 by saying that Jesus gave apostles, prophets, evangelists, pastors, and teachers.

Romans 16:7

Paul greets Andronicus and Junia, his relatives, and calls them outstanding among the apostles. Various respected scholars tell us that Junia was a common female name in Paul's day. Bible commentators were unanimous until the 13th century that Junia was a female name, when the name of Junias, which did not exist in Paul's day, began to be used instead by some translators to imply a male name. The acclaimed 4th century bishop of Constantinople, Chrysostom, wrote of Junia, "Oh how great is the devotion of this woman that she should be counted worthy of the appellation of apostle!" [4]

JOHN

2 John 1, 10

John, one of the original 12 apostles, writes his second letter to "the elect lady," or, as some translations say, "the lady chosen by God" and her "children." John uses the term "children" 19 times in his first two letters to refer to the children of God and refers to himself as a child of God (1 John 3:1-2). In the passage of Scripture to the elect lady, he is giving a warning about false teachers, so the lady was evidently responsible for teachers who might come to her house, as occurred with all the house churches of that time.

NO?
Needs Study to Evaluate

PAUL

The three specific scriptures that have been used by some to put limits on women in ministry all come from Paul. How can this be when we have just seen his strong support for women? Respected scholars have different theories.

I Corinthians 14:34-36

"Women should remain silent in the churches. They are not allowed to speak, but must be in submission, as the law says. If they want to inquire about something, they should ask their own husbands at home; for it is disgraceful for a woman to speak in the church. What? Did the word of God originate with you? Or are you the only people it has reached?" [Revised Standard Version and several other translations.]

FACTS:
- No "law" in the Scriptures prevented women from speaking in church, but Jewish oral law said women must be silent in the synagogues.
- Paul discusses women praying and prophesying earlier in 1 Corinthians 11:5 without rebuke.
- No quotation marks existed in the Greek to know when someone was quoting.
- A one-letter Greek word immediately follows the verses about women being silent that is often used to refute what was just said. Paul uses this word at least 14 times in the book of Corinthians to refute their misunderstandings. [5]
- Paul addresses a rebuke (What?) in verse 36 to the second person masculine, "you men." [6]

SCHOLARS' THEORIES:
1. The women, who did not have the same education their husbands did, were interrupting with too many questions when the prophecies were being weighed (referred to in verse 29); this was too disruptive, and Paul told them to inquire later of their husbands, who had been better educated in that culture, *or*

47

2. Paul is correcting the Corinthian men for not allowing women to speak, given (a) the reference to the "law," (b) the tone of rebuke that Paul uses in the verse immediately following that are addressed just to the men, (c) Paul's mention earlier, without rebuke, of women praying and prophesying, and (d) the presence of the Greek word that Paul often uses to refute the Corinthians' multiple misunderstandings.

1 Corinthians 3:12

"But I want you to realize that the head of every man is Christ, and the head of the woman is man, and the head of Christ is God.... For as woman came from man, so also man is born of woman. But everything comes from God."

FACTS:
- The word *head* can mean "authority" or "origin/source." [7] Much research and debate continues about its meaning in this passage.
- The order Paul uses of man first, woman next and Christ last does not make sense for a meaning of authority.
- Paul refers to the origin/source of men and women just a few verses later in verse 12.

SCHOLARS' THEORIES:
1. Paul is saying that a man is the authority over a woman, *or*
2. Paul is saying that man was the source of woman, as in Eve coming from Adam's side, given that (a) the order given makes sense for source but not authority, (b) Paul repeats similar words with the clear idea of source a few verses later, and (c) that the passage is not about authority. Therefore, Paul would be saying that the source of man is Christ, the source of woman is man (from Adam), and the source of Christ is God.

1 Timothy 2:11-12

"A woman should learn in quietness and full submission. I do not permit a woman to teach or to have authority over a man; she must be quiet. For Adam was formed first, then Eve. And Adam was not the one deceived; it was the woman who was deceived and became a sinner. But women will be saved through childbearing—if they continue in faith, love and holiness with propriety."

FACTS:

- Learning "in quietness and full submission" was a known phrase of the day for the attitude of a good student, a revolutionary concept for women, who were not taught in that day as men were.

- The original Greek word that Paul uses here for "authority" *(authentein)* is not the one normally used in the New Testament for authority *(exousiazo).* [8] In fact, this Greek word is not used anywhere else in the New Testament, and it was rarely used at all in ancient times. Current research shows that this word probably means to "have the upper hand" or be "dominating." [9]

- Paul corrected false teaching repeatedly in the book of First Timothy. Ephesus was a centre of pagan worship, with some teachings that Eve was created before Adam, women were superior to men, and that it was better for women not to have children. [10]

- The Greek verb for "permit" is in the present tense, "I am not *now* permitting...," implying specific instructions for this situation. [11]

SCHOLARS' THEORIES:

1. A woman should not teach or have authority over a man, in particular a married woman over her husband, because Adam was created first, *or*

2. Paul is forbidding women from attempting to dominate men with the pagan teaching of women's superiority and pre-eminence , given that (a) the Greek word Paul used is not the normal word for authority but is always negative and has tones of domination, (b) Paul says he makes his statement because (for) Adam was formed first and the woman was deceived (though Scripture clearly points out that Adam sinned too), which would specifically refute the pagan teaching of Ephesus, (c) Paul begins the passage with the revolutionary concept that a woman should have the opportunity to learn too, which would be the antidote to the false teaching he is continually correcting in his letter, (d) Paul closes with reassurance regarding a believer's surviving childbirth (which could be a sensitive topic for pagan women accustomed to prayer to the fertility goddess), and (e) nowhere else does Paul say that women should not teach or have authority over a man. To the contrary he commends women in ministry such as Phoebe and Priscilla.

* * * * *

OTHER?

Apostles: Some people say that women are restricted from certain forms of ministry because the twelve apostles Jesus selected were all male, however, highly respected scholars have pointed out that Jesus sent the apostles initially to the Jews, who by custom were not supposed to listen to a woman's voice in public or in the synagogue. Scholars also point out that Jesus Himself commissioned a woman first to share the good news that He was risen. [12]

Elders: In 1 Timothy 3, immediately following the passage above regarding Ephesus with its false teaching, Paul lists very strict qualifications for elders that would not even include unmarried men. Some have used this passage to say that women should never be elders or leaders in a church. It is to be noted, however, that in Paul's time, only men were elders in the synagogues, and only men would have had the opportunity for the type of learning that would enable them to be teachers, as Paul required of an elder. Yet it is interesting to note that even in 1 Timothy 3:11, in the context of Ephesus, Paul includes in his passage on leadership, in striking parallel in both words and grammatical structure, the characteristics for godly women (not "their" wives, as some translations incorrectly state). [13]   It should also be noted that Paul called Phoebe a deacon/minister (the Greek *diakonos*), the same Greek word he used to describe himself. [14]

Rulership/submission: Some have used the Fall, and God's statement to Eve that Adam would rule over her, to say that men should always be the leaders. The highly esteemed theologian Roger Nicole points out that God's words were a "divine description of what would occur, not a mandate which obedient servants of God should attempt to carry out." Likewise, he states that the husband/wife relationship described by Scripture refers to a loving relationship in the home and "in no wise precludes the exercise of leadership by women in society and the church." [15]

50

References
1. F.F. Bruce, "Women in the Church: a Biblical Survey," Christian Brethren
   Review, 33: 9.
2. David Joel Hamilton. I Commend to You Our Sister (master's thesis,
   University of the Nations, 1996), Appendix O, 736-739. As cited in Loren
   Cunningham and David J. Hamilton, Why Not Women? (Seattle, WA:
   YWAM Publishing, 2000).
3. John Chrysostom. "First Homily on the Greeting to Priscilla and Aquila,"
   translated by Catherine Clark Kroeger, Priscilla Papers 7.1 (Winter 1993),
   18.
4. The Homilies of St. John Chrysostom, Nicene and Post-Nicene Fathers
   Series 1, 11:555, (Wm. B.Eerdmans, 1956).
5. Thayer's Greek-English Lexicon of the New Testament (Grand Rapids, MI:
   Baker Book House, 1977), # 2228.
6. Gilbert Bilezikian, Beyond Sex Roles (Grand Rapids, MI: Baker Book
   House, 1985), 151.
7. F.F. Bruce, New Century Bible Commentary, 1 and 2 Corinthians (London:
   Marshall, Morgan & Scott, printed in the United States by Grand Rapids,
   MI: Wm. B. Eerdmans, 1971), 103. Gordon D. Fee. The New
   International Commentary on the New Testament, The First Epistle to the
   Corinthians (Grand Rapids, MI: Wm. B. Eerdmans, 1987).
8. Ruth A. Tucker and Walter Liefeld. Daughters of the Church, (Grand
   Rapids, MI: Zondervan, 1987), 460.
9. Catherine Clark Kroeger & Mary J. Evans, eds. The IVP Women's Bible
   Commentary (Downer's Grove, IL: InterVarsity Press, 2002), 741.
10. Kurt Rudolph, The Nature and History of Gnosticism (San Francisco, CA:
    Harper, 1987). See Index/ Woman.
11. Gordon D. Fee, New International Biblical Commentary, 1 and 2 Timothy,
    Titus (Peabody, MA: Hendrickson Publishers, 1984), 72.
12. F.F. Bruce, "Women in the Church: a Biblical Survey," Christian Brethren
    Review, 33: 9. Roger Nicole, "Biblical Concept of Women," Evangelical
    Dictionary of Theology (Grand Rapids, MI:Baker Book House, 1984),
    1177.
13. The IVP Women's Bible Commentary, 743.
14. Thayer's Greek-English Lexicon of the New Testament, # 1249.
15. Roger Nicole, "Biblical Concept of Women," Evangelical Dictionary of
    Theology (Grand Rapids, MI: Baker Book House, 1984), 1176, 1178-
    1179.

Other Sources
A.J. Gordon, "The Ministry of Women," 1894, in J. Robert Clinton, Gender and
Leadership (Altadena, CA: Barnabas Publishers, 1995).
Craig Keener, The IVP Bible Background Commentary, New Testament
    (Downer's Grove, IL: InterVarsity Press, 1993).

Ronald F. Youngblood, ed. <u>Nelson's New Illustrated Bible Dictionary</u>
(Nashville, TN: Thomas Nelson Publishers, 1995).
Howard F. Vos, <u>Nelson's New Illustrated Bible Manners & Customs</u> (Nashville,
TN: Thomas Nelson Publishers, 1999).

3. Are Spiritual Gifts Gender Based?

A. Spiritual Gifts in Missions and Evangelism: On Men and Women, I Will Pour Forth of my Spirit":
Theological Reflections on Spiritual Gifts
by Deborah M. Gill and Barbara L. Cavaness

What about women in the church? What were their roles *then*, in the first churches? What should be their roles *now*, in this day and age? The New Testament spotlights Jesus as the model. He treated women with respect and dignity, included them in spiritual matters and involved them in religious work. New Testament theology — God's words about women and their roles — teaches that the Holy Spirit equips all people (male and female) for God's work. New Testament history depicts the first-century church at worship. It describes women as full participants in the services, equal recipients of spiritual gifts, and leaders at all levels — even identifying female ministers by the same titles as their male counterparts.

The New Testament lists three categories of spiritual gifts in three passages of Scripture. Though each category is distinct in its purposes, all gifts share the following elements:

a) Each gift represents a unique way God's grace *enables* individuals to effectively do His work in the world and in the Church.

b) God's gifts are not given as badges of honour to those who deserve them, but are *unmerited* gifts of grace.

c) Spiritual gifts are given for the common good, that is, to serve the needs of *others*, for the building up of the body of Christ, and for ministry in the marketplace.

d) Thus, all gifts are to be operated with *love*.[1]

e) God has poured out His Spirit on sons and daughters alike, equipping *both genders* in every category of gifts.

Supernatural Gifts: 1 Corinthians 12-14
First Corinthians 12-14 discusses the nine *supernatural* gifts of the Spirit: a message of wisdom, a message of knowledge, faith, gifts of healing, miraculous powers, prophecy, distinguishing between spirits,

---

[1] Note that in close proximity to all three gifts passages is an emphasis on love (1 Cor. 13:1-13, Rom. 12:9-12, and Eph. 4:15).

speaking in different kinds of tongues and the interpretation of tongues. The Holy Spirit makes the choice of which gifts He gives to which individuals (1Corinthians 12:11), and those spiritually-gifted persons comprise God's gifts to the Church. *"God has placed the parts [in this context, spiritually-gifted people] in the body, every one of them, just as he wanted them to be"* (1Corinthians 12:18). Gender has no bearing on the choices He makes.

The members of the body of Christ and their spiritual gifts are diverse, yet together they form a unified whole. God's plan is that *"there should be no division in the body"* (1Corinthians 12:25). Every part (person, including their gifts) is needed; every part is to be valued; every part is to be honoured and cared for — and every believer is a part of the Body (1Corinthians 12:27). Scripture warns against devaluing God's gifts (1Thessalonians 5:20; 1Corinthians 14:39).

The gifts are so beneficial to the Church that Scripture encourages all of Christ's followers to seek them, especially certain gifts. Paul writes, *"Eagerly desire the greater gifts;"* that is, *"those [gifts] that build up the church,"* and *"eagerly desire spiritual gifts, especially the gift of prophecy"* (1Corinthians 12:31; 14:1, 12 [compare 6-11]). *"Therefore, my brothers and sisters, be eager to prophesy"* (1Corinthians 14:39). If the apostle Paul is suggesting any ranking of supernatural gifts, the "greater" gift seems to be prophecy.

Prophecy is a spiritual gift with which the Holy Spirit gifted women in the New Testament (1Corinthians 11:5). First Corinthians 11:5 says that prophesying women were active in the worship service. Female prophets were among those the Holy Spirit gave to the New Testament church (Acts 21:9). Scripture explains that though not every person is a prophet (1Corinthians 12:29), *any* person (male or female) can be gifted by the Holy Spirit to prophesy (1Corintians 14:31). Furthermore, prophets are authorized to judge the authenticity of utterance gifts (1Corinthians 14:29). Thus those who prophesy have authority in the supernatural gifts. Since the Holy Spirit gifted women in the New Testament with prophecy — perhaps the highest of supernatural gifts — it follows that all the rest of the supernatural gifts are available to women as well.

Motivational Gifts: Romans 12:3-8

Like spiritual temperaments, the motivational gifts are the inner inclinations that influence why individuals think and act the way they do. They are the very core of what motivates a person.

These motivations are graciously given by God to each member of the Body in order to serve Him with joy. For example, the motivational gift of prophesying involves a drive to perceive the will of God and speak it out to others. Serving involves the joy of helping meet the needs of others. Teaching involves a love for research and communicating truth in an effort to see lives changed. Encouraging involves being a positive influence to help people live victoriously. Giving involves finding joy in investing resources to benefit others and advance the gospel. Leading involves thriving on organizing, facilitating, and directing. Showing mercy involves the desire to heal hurting hearts.

To paraphrase the apostle Paul, "*Whatever your motivation, exercise it for all you're worth!*" (Romans 12:6-8). All Christ's followers, male and female, have been graciously gifted with unique motivations.[ii] It grieves the Holy Spirit to see the passionate involvement of a person He had spiritually motivated rejected by the body of Christ.

Equipping Gifts: Ephesians 4:4-16

Ephesians 4:4-16 discusses the *equipping* gifts. Scripture specifies that it is the grace that Christ gives to a believer (Ephesians 4:7) that qualifies him or her to be Christ's gift to the Church. The five[iii] gifts (sometimes called "offices") are identified as apostles, prophets, evangelists, pastors and teachers. God gives grace to meet the Church's needs with these gifts through the people God sends as their leaders. These leaders' work is to equip the members of the Body for ministry, so that the Church might grow in unity, orthodoxy[iv] and maturity —growing into complete Christ-likeness. Apostles establish works for God. Prophets speak as mouthpieces for God. (A person who prophesies with regularity and is judged to be accurate and anointed may come to be recognized as a prophet.) Evangelists proclaim the "good news," helping

---

[ii] Don and Katie Fortune, <u>Discovering Your God-given Gifts</u> (Grand Rapids, MI: Chosen Books, 1987), 16.
[iii] It may be more accurate to count the equipping gifts as four since the Greek text seems to identify "pastor-teachers" as one spiritual gift to the Church.
[iv] Orthodoxy: accurate or right teaching, conforming to established doctrine.

people come to Jesus in salvation. Pastors care for the flock of God. Teachers train the flock of God.

In the New Testament, the highest spiritual leadership gift is an apostle. If a woman could serve as an apostle, it would follow that she could serve in any other office. Were there any women apostles in the New Testament? Yes, Junia in Romans 16:7.

What is the New Testament theology of spiritual gifts and women? Robert Clinton, noted author on leadership, concludes that *"both males and females can lead and exercise leadership with gifted power."*[v] The New Testament teaches that those gifted by God are responsible to employ their gifts for one another as good stewards of God's great grace (1 Peter 4:10).

Destined to become one of the great female evangelists, Maria Underwood [Woodworth-Etter] felt God's call at age thirteen (1858). She said,

I heard the voice of Jesus calling me to go out in the highways and hedges and gather in the lost sheep... I had never heard of women working in public except as missionaries, so I could see no opening — except as I thought, if I ever married, my choice would be an earnest Christian and then we would enter upon the mission field.[vi]

Her marriage to an ex-soldier/farmer did not result in ministry, so she struggled with her call. They lost five of their six children to illnesses before Maria's rededication to the Lord in 1879. She was "baptized with the Holy Ghost, and fire."[vii] Still she hesitated and tried to study further, even as she prayed for her husband's permission to go out in ministry. In her struggle, she thought, "If I were a man it would be a pleasure for me, but for me, a woman, to preach, if I could, would subject me to ridicule and contempt ... and bring reproach upon our glorious cause."[viii] After seeing a vision of Jesus, finding examples in

---

[v] J. Robert Clinton, Gender and Leadership: My Pilgrimage (Altadena, CA: Barnabas Publishers, 1995), 12, 20.

[vi] Maria Woodworth, Life and Experience of Maria B. Woodworth (Dayton, OH: United Brethren, 1885), 18.

[vii] Maria Woodworth-Etter, Signs and Wonders God Wrought in the Ministry for Forty Years rep. ed. (Bartlesville, OK: Oak Tree, 1916), 28.

[viii] Woodworth, 38.

the Bible of how God used women to lead and studying Acts 2, Maria was convinced that "women are required to work for the advancement of Christ's cause." [ix]

She began holding revival meetings in Ohio and planting churches. During the first year and a half, she "held four revivals, organized two churches — one of them with about seventy members — and a Sabbath-school of about one hundred scholars ... had preached in twenty-two meeting houses and four school-houses, for eight different denominations and had delivered two hundred sermons." [x]

In 1885 Maria Woodworth began conducting healing services as well, eventually travelling widely with an 8,000-seat tent, attracting publicity and winning converts around the country. She remained a highly respected evangelist in the Pentecostal movement the rest of her life.

In her autobiography, *Signs and Wonders God Wrought in the Ministry for Forty Years,* Woodworth-Etter explains the reason for her bold obedience to God: *"When a woman is called by God, how can she be obedient without answering the call? How can you doubt the call when God himself confirms it with miraculous power?"* [xi] She used the same logic the first-century apostles and elders used to conclude that Gentiles may become Christ's followers — the evidence of the Holy Spirit's work of grace and power (Acts 15:6, 7-9, 12). How did the Jerusalem Council perceive that God makes no distinctions between people? They witnessed God's grace in salvation and God's power in signs and wonders. So they concluded, *"We should not make it difficult for the Gentiles who are turning to God"* (Acts 15:19).

As the first church concluded, may today's church also say, "We should not make it difficult for the women who are obeying God."

[ix] Woodworth-Etter, 41.
[x] Woodworth-Etter, 54.
[xi] Woodworth-Etter, 30-31.

B. Adaptation of a Parable
By Cecilia Yau

I would like to begin with an example, which illustrates the problem of limiting women's spiritual gifts in any cultural context.

A man going on a journey called all his servants and entrusted his property to them. To one maidservant he gave five talents of money, to another two talents, and to another one talent, each according to her ability. Then he went on his journey. The maidservant who had received one talent went at once and put her money to work and gained one more.

The one with the two talents was looked upon with suspicion. People told her, "For women, the lesser the talents, the more virtuous they are. Women are emotional, they can't be trusted with talents." As a result, she buried one talent and put the other talent to work and gained one more. The maidservant with the five talents could not believe what she got. The Master must have made a mistake! The head-servant also warned her that it was against the will of the Master for a woman to use the five talents. In submission she buried the five talents.

After a long time the Master returned and settled accounts with all His servants. The maidservant with one talent brought the other one talent. "Master, you entrusted me with one talent. See, I have gained one more." Her Master replied, "Well done, good and faithful servant. Come and share your Master's happiness."

The maidservant with the two talents also came. "Master, you gave me two talents but I know I only deserve one. I was told the extra talent was your test of my humility and modesty as a woman. So I buried one and used the other to gain one more." Her Master was displeased and replied, "You unfaithful servant! Why did you put more trust in man's word than in my words? I was going to put you in charge of many things. But now you have lost the chance."

Then the maidservant with five talents came. "Master," she said, "I knew you had made woman to be inferior to man and that she should submit to him. So I went out and buried your talents in the ground. See, here is what belongs to you." The Master replied, "You foolish servant! Didn't I tell you that each one of you shall be accountable for what I have entrusted to you? Why did you honour man and fear him more than me? Take away her talents and throw her outside, into the darkness, where there will be weeping and gnashing of teeth."

At last, the Master called the head-servant and rebuked him, "You wicked servant! Why did you stop others from faithfully using their gifts to build up my church? Take him away and throw him outside, into the darkness where there will be weeping and gnashing of teeth."

What Keeps Women From Using Their Gifts?
Why are women hindered from using their God-given gifts in the cause of Christ? What is the mentality that causes this to happen? There are several possibilities. Let me outline a few below:

1. The Role Model Theory:
In the Role Theory Model, Men are not accustomed to seeing women as leaders. (Of course this assumption is becoming obsolete in today's society). They would be turned off or think that religion is a womanly thing. This would discourage men from opening up to the gospel.

Since there are generally more women than men in most churches, one way to increase the number of men is to have more male role models. If female leaders turn off men, then women should hold back or refrain from their more visible roles in order to encourage men to get involved.

A sister who has a gift in preaching and teaching decided to hold back. She refused to take the responsibility of preaching when she was a Christian Education minister. She thought that would encourage brothers to rise up to the leadership role. What she did not realize was that she discouraged many sisters from developing their gifts for the Kingdom. Today there are many more male than female leadership role models. Yet the number of men in the pews has not changed much. However, we do see many women who are afraid to fully utilize their gifts for the Lord.

2. The Leadership Complex Theory
With the Leadership Complex Theory, men feel that they have to be leaders, at least over women; therefore seeing women as leaders, they may feel intimidated or inadequate, thus discouraged from serving. An ordained Chinese woman pastor is having a phenomenal growth in her

church both in terms of members and the church building. The church just moved into a 20-million-plus building project. Her sermon tapes are widely circulated even outside her church. She has two female associate pastors. All three are women, but somehow those who are attracted to the church are mainly women, particularly those who come from broken families. This may confirm some of the above theories. Nevertheless, the problem may be that their leadership is only one gender. Changing into a dual-gender leadership may improve the situation. Yet it may be hard to find men who do not have a leadership gift.

3. The Blaming Game Theory

In the Blaming Game Theory, men tend to see women as sex objects. For women, particularly young women, to stand before men (to preach) or to be in the spot light may confuse the message.

In a denominational convention, a special session was set apart to discuss women in ministry. After the presentation by a woman pastor who was obviously egalitarian, the floor was open for discussion. Someone pointed out that the Chinese churches in North America are increasingly dominated by mainland China immigrants who are used to women in leadership. Immediately a pastor commented that a current American church problem is that "many pastors are involved in pornography. They look at women as sex objects so it is very hard for them to see women in positions of spiritual leadership." If this is true, it is all the more problematic (and dangerous too) for men to pastor congregations — at least half of which are sex objects!

4. The Cultural Habit Theory

With the Cultural Habit Theory, people in general, including women, do not take women as seriously as men. People listen more to male leaders, submit more to them. Even female followers do that. It is harder for female leaders to achieve the same results as male leaders even if they have the same qualifications.

A woman minister complains that she is not taken as authoritatively as her male counterparts. For example, if she visits a sick member in the hospital, before she leaves, the patient sometimes asks: "When will the 'pastor' come to pray for me?" But she is their pastor! However, she does not have the title because she is not ordained. Another woman member always gives Christmas offerings to the male "pastors" in the church but not the female pastors. The women ministers' words are not taken as final; people always want to know what the (male) "pastor" thinks. Having considered these theories, may I suggest that women on the whole lack self-confidence because of the long-standing biases against them. Furthermore, with the deep-rooted cultural habits of the people in the congregation, women are discouraged from exercising their leadership gifts. Because of the subtle responses from people, many women truly believe they do not have leadership gifts.

People use all kinds of excuses to keep women from fully exercising their God-given gifts. This sends a wrong message to non-Christians who are used to equality of genders at home and at their work place. I was once invited to speak to a group of scholars from China who were doing research at University of California, Berkeley. Some were quite ready to accept the gospel except for one consideration. They had observed that both the Bible and the church seem to look down on women. They were alarmed that women are barred from preaching and leadership roles. They wondered if God really meant it that way.

I came from the West Coast of the U.S.A. In the area where I serve, there are approximately 300,000 Chinese and about 170 Chinese churches. About one-third of the churches are looking for pastors. There are ads in Chinese Christian periodicals on positions open. I once talked to one of the leaders of a search committee about accepting a female candidate.

He flatly told me they would only consider male candidates. I asked him why and he said there were just no qualified women. In his own experience, he had come across women who were too emotional and unstable, had not much vision and majored on the minors. I asked him if he had come across bad apples in men's group and would he come to the same conclusion about men. In fact the church where he was the head deacon had just fired the senior pastor, a man. He obviously applies a double standard. Like him, many church boards prefer to go without shepherds rather than having a female pastor.

As China began to incorporate the truth that women and men are equally gifted to minister, a wonderful season of fruitfulness ensued. Allowing and encouraging both men and women to exercise all their gifts can only benefit the cause of evangelism and missions.

During the early 20th century, China was swept by waves of revivals. Many great preachers were born. Not a few of them were women. One, named Dora Yu, was anointed with the power of the Holy Spirit. Through her preaching, many came to the Lord. Among them were the famous Watchman Nee and Witness Lee. She also founded a Bible school. Two other women established the Bethel Seminary and trained many future servants of the Lord. Christiana Tsai and other leaders started the Chinese Home Missionary Society with many evangelists, both women and men, travelling to different cities to preach the gospel in remote places in China. Other women taught at the seminaries and wrote commentaries.

However as history repeats itself, once the Chinese Church was well established with hierarchical structure, women were once again marginalized. It is ironic that the indigenous Chinese church movement started by Watchman Nee and later led also by Witness Lee today forbids women in leadership roles.

For almost 50 years, women within the church were "silenced'" and pushed back behind the scene. Then came the Communist Era; churches went underground. In late 70's, the iron curtain of China was pulled back. The Church emerged. The growth of the church jumped 100-fold. A lot of the new Christians are in the countryside. A majority of them are women. Everywhere teams of Christian women travel up the hills and down the fields, toiling side by side with the farm workers doing evangelism. They also host and lead house churches. Many of them also have to teach the Bible even though they do not have much Biblical knowledge.

Up to now, there is still open opportunity for women in China to use their gifts for the Lord. Will the door close once again when the Church in China becomes stabilized and institutionalized?

4. Empowering Men and Women in Ministry- Partnerships

A. Models of Women in Ministry Around the World Today

by Cosmas Ilechukwu, Rev. Dorothy Colney and Uma David

The following are case studies of women using their spiritual gifts and finding opportunities to advance the gospel in Nigeria, Myanmar and India.

NIGERIA, by Pastor Cosmas Ilechukwu

The gifts, talents, skills, and opportunities God has allowed to each person should determine ministry roles in the body of Christ. God is very economical in his gifting. He is not likely to waste his gift on any person for whom he does not have a job. One proof that God wants women in ministry alongside men is that they are as gifted as men.

In Nigeria, we have many successful women in ministries who serve as models. They all share a few common traits:

- They all discovered their gifts and worked hard to develop them.
- They are strongly committed to their families and see their families as their first responsibility.
- They have a healthy view of men, seeing them not as competitors but as indispensable partners in ministry.
- They are committed to equipping others, not to controlling them.

Bishop Margaret Benson-Idahusa is currently presiding bishop of one of the biggest Pentecostal churches in Africa — the Church of God Mission International. Her husband, Archbishop Benson Idahusa, founded this church. After his death in 1998, she became presiding bishop. The pastors all agree she has the gift of leadership. One said, "her outstanding success in ministry lies in her ability to motivate people and help them to fulfil their potential." The numerous ministries of the church now include a university, which is rated one of the best in Nigeria.

Dr. Love Amaga, the wife of Bishop Sam Amaga of the Foundation Faith International Churches. A gifted teacher and conference speaker, she works to restore biblical family values. A prolific writer, she has published several books on family life and other topics.

Mrs. Folu Adeboye, the wife of the General Overseer of the Redeemed Christian Church of God. As a gifted encourager, she mentors women in ministry and the wives of ministers. The impact of her work has been tremendous.

Pastor Adeola Ilechukwu, an outstanding Bible teacher, is in popular demand in churches and conferences in Nigeria. She serves as executive director for the African Centre for Christian Leadership. Her particular burden is helping women improve their self-esteem as a prelude to fulfilling the mandate of God on their lives.

Conclusion:
Because women are called "helpers" in the Bible, they must be understood in the sense used to describe God in Psalm 54:4. *"Surely God is my help; the Lord is the one who sustains me."* Women are to help from strength and not from weakness, therefore women should be viewed as mutual partners with men in ministry. Mutuality between men and women in ministry is necessary because each has strengths and weaknesses. Each needs the other for completeness and fulfilment. God does not want His gifts, whether in men or women, to be wasted. Our emphasis should be on making the most of all that God has given to the church to His utmost glory.

MYANMAR by Rev. Dorothy Colney
I am currently regional leader for Women of Global Action for S.E. Asia. I have translated Campus Crusade for Christ materials into Burmese and served as a pastor of Church of God in Myanmar (Evangelical), preaching, teaching and evangelizing. I have baptized more than 100 converts from other religions — Buddhists, Hindus, Muslims. Here are some of the women leaders I have met in my country.

Miss Esther Say Phaw is a prayer warrior, missionary to the Salone people, Bible translator and inventor of the script of the Salone language. Salone people are known as "sea gypsies" who live in houseboats in the summer and on islands the rest of the year. Miss Esther moved to one of the islands where she built a small church and a school for children. She taught the children to read in their own

64

language. She translated the New Testament into Salone language and has begun work on the Old Testament.

Dr. Khin Than Thay was born into a family of teachers. She went to college and eventually earned a Ph.D. degree. Dr. Khin Than Thay taught in secondary schools for many years, moving with her husband in his government appointments. She helped to begin a Bible college. She later studied communication techniques and taught them to groups around the world. Dr. Khin now serves as evangelist for Immanuel City Mission Karen Church and helps to organize evangelistic tours to the villages where many unbelievers live. She helps direct the annual Festival of Praise with more than 60 churches participating, and more than 3,000 attending.

Rev. Dr. Khuang Nawni is general director and co-founder of the Christian Baptist Church of Myanmar. The association of Christian Baptist Churches has now grown to 73 churches in Yangon area. She and her husband began seven new churches and realized the need for a school to train local leaders. To get government permission, they agreed that she should get an advanced degree, since she had more education than her husband. She earned a Master of Divinity degree from a seminary in the Philippines, and eventually a Ph.D. from Fuller Theological seminary in USA. Her husband encouraged and supported her.

Today Dr. Nawni and her husband lead a team of rural evangelists, pastor a church in the slums of Yangon, and run an orphanage and school for 62 children.

Rev. Agnes Daw Hia Yin is senior pastor and founder of Kyauk-Yay-Twin Faith Church in Myanmar and president of the executive committee of Women for Global Action (Myanmar). For several years she was on the full-time staff of Campus Crusade for Christ and many new converts were added to churches in the area. Eventually she felt led by God to start a church of her own. After several difficult years of renting places and much opposition from other groups, she found places to meet and eventually secured a building. Her congregation grew to 400, plus four outreaches that total about 200 new converts.

INDIA by Uma David

India has more than a billion people, hundreds of languages and dialects, class and cast systems, different religions, customs and traditions.

Women and children, especially girls, are considered less than human. Girl babies are often killed or abandoned in dust bins. A girl is a liability because the father incurs huge debts to get her married with an elaborate wedding and heavy dowry paid to the groom's family.

India's technological growth is stupendous, and education is now available, but most rural people live in ignorance. Even educated people hang on to old customs, traditions, and superstitions. Against this backdrop, we will consider two remarkable women.

Shanti Solomon was born into a Hindu family, but her parents became believers in Christ. Her father died when she was six weeks old and her mother was then driven from her ancestral home by her Hindu in-laws. Her mother supported the family of three children and helped Shanti get an education. Shanti married a Christian man, they had no children and he died after ten years. As a result of a vision from God, she began the Fellowship of the Least Coin — a global movement of prayer for peace, justice, and reconciliation. Each member commits to spend time in prayer whenever she has a strained relationship with another person. The members also agree to pray for victims of jealousy, hatred, violence and injustice. Each time a member prays, she sets aside a "least coin" as a token of her prayer. The amount is chosen by the local group, being sure that the poorest woman in the group can participate. The amount collected is never publicized because it is not a fund-raising project but a movement of prayer for peace and reconciliation.

The "least coins" go to the FLC Custodial Fund in Geneva, Switzerland, from which a committee gives project grants to 30 or 40 programs around the world. Today, women from more than 80 countries participate in the Fellowship of the Least Coin.

Augusta Noble has begun an effective intercessory prayer ministry. Brought up in a Christian home, she married and had three children, living in a beautiful house. After her husband became ill, they had to sell their home to maintain a living and educate their children.

Then her eldest son was stricken with leukemia and died at age 13. She began putting her troubles behind her and praying for others. Then she contracted cancer of the lymph nodes and prolonged treatment weakened her, but her sick husband still needed her care. Unable to leave the house, she began a prayer ministry through the phone. People of all faiths began to call her asking for prayer.

Through her prayers she has brought much-needed comfort and hope to the many people who call day and night asking for help.

Conclusion

As women find opportunities to use their God-given gifts and abilities alongside men, they are making new inroads in missions and evangelism. We celebrate the creative, intelligent and faithful ways women use their gifts in advancing Christ's kingdom. The harvest is ripe. The labourers are ready. Christian women are gifted and impassioned to serve and they have found new ways of serving, even in cultures that restrict women.

B. How Culture Affects the Roles of Women and Men in Ministry

by Judy Mbugua, E. Leevathi Manasse, Nora Matilde Mendez de Mora and Russell Palsrok

In exploring the cultural impact of gender on ministry, examples from Kenya, India, Venezuela and the United States were selected as case studies, illustrating the impact of gender on Christian ministry.

AFRICA by Judy W. Mbugua, PACWA Continental Coordinator (Kenya, Africa)

The Oxford Dictionary defines culture as "the customs, civilization and achievement of a particular time or people." Culture often determines the values, worldview, attitudes, behaviour and practices of women and men from birth to death. Understanding culture is important in considering how we might best approach the issue of gender in Christian ministry. Only then can one determine an effective strategy for recreating the desired values, norms and practices.

Although most cultures look down upon women, and up to men, they express it differently. In Africa, where I live, when a man visits a home and the husband/father is not in, the visitor goes away saying there was nobody at home — even though the wife (or wives) were there and were hospitable to him. In one mosque in Nairobi, Kenya, a notice pinned outside reads: "Women and dogs are not allowed in the Mosque."

Traditional African society looked upon women as perpetually dependent on males. Women have to be protected and guided by men. Women are often objects of exploitation, and a source of wealth to men who handle them like personal property.

Yet, despite this cultural subordination, women in African tradition frequently occupy leading positions in divining, rainmaking and as mediums in prophesying, healing and counselling. These occupations illustrate that women *are* given leadership in various spheres, even in cultures generally repressive towards women.

Examples of African Culture and the Treatment of Women

- *Chicken Wings* — In Uganda, women cannot eat chicken wings. Otherwise they would fly like a chicken and not be submissive, especially in bed.
- *Physical Abuse* — In some cultures in West Africa, women are to be beaten at least once in three months in order to remain disciplined. If they are not beaten, the women ask for it!
- *Female Genital Mutilation (FGM)*. Some cultures say that a woman needs to go through FGM to be tamed, so that she does not become sexually promiscuous. This primitive practice is still active. The Kenya Demographic Health Survey of 1998 indicated that 50% of women aged 35 years and above are circumcised!

While most cultures seem to lower or reduce the value of women, at the same time culture often raises the value for men to threatening proportions. For example, a Moran (Maasai young man) is expected to kill a lion to prove he is a real man. The boy child is encouraged "never to cry."

Marriage and Concubines in Botswana and Swaziland

Polygamy is tolerated and some pastors have a wife in the rural areas and another in the city. This is especially true for itinerant evangelists who are allowed to keep concubines in different cities where they go to preach.

Wife Inheritance

Some men put aside their Christian perspectives in order to seize the properties and wife of a deceased brother in the name of culture, even when the husband dies of HIV/AIDS. Knowing that the wife was infected, men said they would rather die of HIV/AIDS than break their culture!

The Church

These traditions and cultures have found their way into the church's attitude toward men and women in spite of Jesus' teaching in Matthew 15:6, *"Thus you nullify the word of God for the sake of your tradition."* The word of God has often been sacrificed at the altar of culture and tradition.

Discrimination Against Women in Ordination

Whereas women are allowed to take the same courses with men in Bible Colleges, they are not ordained at the end of their training. Churches oversee ordination and most of them do not support women in ministry.

The churches have used and twisted religious doctrines against women. Women must be silent in church. They are supposed to be saved through child bearing. These teachings not only imply that men are superior to women, they also make it difficult for women to succeed in ministry.

The Way Forward

The church, as the company of God's people, should be a redemptive force amid oppressive traditions and culture. The church should provide a supportive environment for women's development.

The church should recognize existing capabilities of women and men. This recognition should help both men and women in their Christian service.

Women are in the majority in our Christian communities. Unfortunately, they have internalized the very myth of inferiority that keeps them from pursuing church ministry. Women must therefore, "restore their dignity, appreciate themselves, be proud of their

69

womanhood and motherhood." In Pan African Women's Association we say that we, "assert our true dignity as found in the Bible!"

Conclusion

There is the saying that "unity is strength." If the church taught the gospel in a way that shows its superiority over negative culture, many men and women would be delivered and empowered towards finishing the task of the Great Commission.

INDIA by E. Leelavathi Manasse, Bangalore

Shanti and her husband Raj are blessed with a daughter and a son. A few years ago, Raj had a personal encounter with Christ in a home Bible study conducted by their church youth group. In one session, they had a discussion on the Christian attitude toward dowry. Dowry, in most parts of our country, is a demanded gift from the father or parents of the bride.

As Raj was reflecting on the issue of dowry, he was convicted by the Holy Spirit to tell Shanti he was sorry for having demanded and taken dowry from her father at the time of their marriage. Shanti was happy about the transformation in Raj's attitude. She explained to Raj the difficulties her father had in borrowing the money and clearing the debt. After discussion and prayer, Raj visited her father to say he was sorry and to return the dowry.

Often we meet people feeling sorry about taking or giving dowry, but seldom do we meet people who actually return the dowry. But this action is a valuable contribution to reshaping and restructuring the world, beginning with our immediate family relationships and our own life. Raj's relationship with Christ changed his outlook on dowry as practiced in his culture. Often we fail to take a bold step to redeem persons and situations from inequality, and injustice. In our new community in Christ, men and women can work side by side, learn from each other, and support one another in restoring the dignity of those who have been marginalized in the family, church, and society.

VENEZUELA by Nora Matilde Mendez de Mora

I have observed the following cultural impediments to mutuality in men and women in ministry in my country of Venezuela.

1. Women are not given encouragement or opportunities by the male pastors who mentor them. It is assumed that women are limited in leadership gifts. A friend told me of one church in a denomination that did not permit women to teach men, even though the women far surpassed the men in Bible knowledge. The leaders finally decided to let two women speak to each other behind a curtain, so the men could listen "by accident."

2. Latin American women are often left alone with a household of children. The Latin culture has insisted that motherhood is the highest and most satisfying state. Motherhood is celebrated through literature, art, religion and national holidays, and this gives rise to matriarchy, dominance and control rather than healthy communication. It also contributes to resentment, co-dependency and fear.

3. Abusive and dysfunctional family systems are common in Latin America. This makes women vulnerable to abuse from shame-based, legalistic churches. We need grace-based models of church life that lend dignity, respect, and opportunities for service to all.

4. Men and women in Christ need to learn how to enjoy true friendship as they grow together in the pursuit of God.

Cultural influences and socialization are powerful impediments to healthy communication required in any profession or ministry. Moreover, cultural influences also perpetuate abuse within the church, home and society.

UNITED STATES by Dr. Russell Palsrok—Christian Reformed Church of North America

The Christian Reformed Church (CRC) has always believed that both men and women are gifted for ministry. However, it is generally assumed that women are gifted for ministry in the home, while men are gifted for ministry in church and society. Women have not been permitted to enter into official ministry positions, yet they often provide significant ministry to the church. They teach children, lead music, organize Bible studies and engage in outreach ministry.

The CRC culture has been ambivalent toward women participating in formal leadership roles. While there was consensus that

71

women should minister, there was division over whether women in ministry are to be subordinate or equal partners with men.

The debate raged back and forth until 1995, when the denomination (in compromise) declared that both positions appear to be biblically defensible from a Reformed hermeneutical viewpoint. Therefore, the decisions about women in ministry positions should be made at the local church level. Consequently, women are given ambivalent messages by the denomination. They may attend seminary and become ordained ministers in the CRC, yet many churches oppose them. Women answer God's call with little assurance they will have a place to serve.

In spite of this, the level of participation and the use of women's gifts have increased during these last ten years. Attitudes are slowly changing from subordination to equality, from repression of women in certain situations to empowerment.

In the regional body in which I serve, women are not permitted to teach, to preach, to administer the sacraments, or to exercise pastoral care as an elder. Women elders cannot be delegates to regional meetings. We are not able to encourage women in our congregations to seek ordination locally. They must transfer to another region that will support them.

In my church, we nominate elders and deacons without gender consideration. Both male and female ministers have preached the word and administered the sacraments. However, this is a first generation change. Many confess to some personal discomfort. Some acknowledge they do not treat males and females equally. We are still too conscious of the issue to function in a completely gender-inclusive environment.

Neither have we been able to discuss what unique gifts a woman might possess that a man may not have. Not acknowledging the sexuality of the woman, we do not ask what contribution motherhood might make to ministry. Perhaps we also treat male ministers as neuter rather than masculine.

Conclusion

The culture of my denomination regarding women in ministry ranges from discouragement to encouragement. Some women are comfortable with subordinate positions; others are impatient with the slow progress toward equal partnership. Some leave the denomination to serve elsewhere. Others struggle with the ambiguity.

This is likely true around the world. Cultural effects, while specific to each setting, are complex, positive and negative. And it may always be that way. Finding the right balance to encourage the church and to advance God's kingdom is ultimately more important than focusing on gender. As we minister from the viewpoint of Kingdom culture, may we transform culture to become more Christ-like.

Conclusion to Research Papers

It has been said that most cultures and religious systems value men more than women. As Christians, we hold that God values all people equally and we seek to become culturally sensitive to the subtle and overt ways culture devalues individuals. We seek to offer a proper and biblical voice that claims, as the Bible does, that all people are created in God's image and therefore all people deserve equal dignity and care.

C. Fishers of People! Cast the Net of the Kingdom!
by Chad and Leslie Neal Segraves

Introduction: *"I in them and you in me. May they be brought to complete unity to let the world know that you sent me and have loved them even as you have loved me."* (John 17:23)

A Jewish teacher of the law asked Jesus, "What is the greatest commandment?" Before Jesus answered this question, He spoke the *Shema*, the greatest Hebrew expression of the oneness of God. *"'Hear, O Israel, the Lord your God is One.' Love the Lord your God with all your heart and with all your soul and with all your mind and with all your strength"* (Mark 12:29-31).

The word "One" which Jesus used to describe the unity and oneness of the Trinity is the same word He uses in John 17 to describe the unity of his followers. Jesus also used the same word "one" in Matthew 19:5-6 to describe the unity and the oneness between a husband and wife *"the two will become one flesh. So they are no longer two, but one...*" Thus, Jesus declared that He expects all believers, including husbands and wives, to seek the unity seen in the Trinity!

The result of unity between a husband and a wife and between believers is not merely for good relationships! Rather unity among believers will *"Let the world know."*

To help believers live this unity, the Bible offers some "one another" principles. The basis for these "one another" principles is LOVE – Love for God and love for people. These "one another" principles are exemplified in the Trinity revealing a perfect relationship among the three Persons.

Scripture reveals the key principles for male and female unity. A few of the MUTUAL actions are as follows:
- *Love* – John 13:34 "...Love **one another**."
- *Service* – Galatians 5:13 "... Serve **one another** in love."
- *Honour* – Romans 12:10 "...Honour **one another** above yourselves."
- *Respect* – 1 Peter 2:17 "Show proper respect to **everyone**..."
- *Submission* - Ephesians 5:21 "Submit to **one another** out of reverence for Christ."

If believers took these commands seriously the world would soon know God's love but as it stands now, over two billion people on earth have little or no access to this truth.

The Net of the Kingdom
Jesus calls His followers "fishers of people" (Mark 1:17) because they are to seek and bring people into God's kingdom. Jesus also compares the kingdom of God to a net, "*Once again, the kingdom of heaven is like a net that was let down into the lake and caught all kinds of fish.*" (Matthew 13:47)

There is only ONE Body of Christ; thus both men and women must hold this net together. As they harvest together, the Body is God's diversity on display. God gives spiritual gifts to ALL believers (Ephesians 4:7), but NEVER are these gifts based on gender.

Yet, some believers seek to limit the opportunities for women to use their God-given gifts. The results of this exclusion and inequality are disastrous. If men hold onto their net, but women drop their part of the net, what happens? FISH GET OUT!

Some believers believe and live as if men are over women. If men seek to hold their net higher than women hold theirs, what happens? Stress, struggle, and disunity occur as we focus on one another instead of the harvest and FISH GET OUT!

Empowering women to serve alongside men is NOT simply "a women's issue." When we allow God to work in believers' lives and empower both men and women to use all their gifts, regardless of gender, we exemplify practical unity that will move the gospel of Christ powerfully through the nations!

Holes in the Net
When men and women are not allowed to use their gifts as God has given them, large holes are ripped in the harvesting net. A few "holes in the net" are listed below:

Theological
- Misunderstanding and misapplying biblical passages regarding gender.
- Misunderstanding how to live as a kingdom citizen.
- Misunderstanding the character and image of God. A view of the Trinity which sees a hierarchy in the Trinity and then applies this heresy to the home and church.
- An incomplete understanding of the cross and redemption, and how relationships are restored.
- Active spiritual war by spiritual powers against men and women.

Societal/Psychological
- Women and men who refuse to believe God can use women, especially in ways that go against cultural practices.
- Men and women who actively promote a hierarchical view of men and women.
- Generally speaking – the increased pride of men and the lower self-esteem of women.
- People in positions of power who are not always willing to release and empower others.

Practical

- Many women have never seen models of women using certain gifts nor models of women in ministry, nor models of men and women in ministry-partnerships. Therefore women never learn that they CAN exercise certain spiritual gifts.
- Ignorance, fear, shame, spiritual attack, physical oppression, spiritual oppression, communal expectations, lack of opportunity, lack of education and lack of power.

Mend the Net

To mend the net, correct biblical teaching is crucial to restore the net so we can catch a greater harvest. All believers need to study and reflect on five main issues.

1. The Trinity

Who is God? How do the Persons of the Trinity relate to one another in community? Throughout church history, major theologians have insisted that the Father, Son, and Holy Spirit are co-eternal and co-equal. There is NO hierarchy in the Trinity. These questions form the starting point from which all other relationships can be studied and practiced.

2. The Kingdom of God

Jesus came announcing the Kingdom of God. He demonstrated kingdom culture, principles, and actions. As citizens of this kingdom, believers must learn to live the kingdom culture even when it contradicts their own culture. Believers need to regain Jesus' emphasis on the kingdom of God.

3. Justice

The foundation of God's throne is justice and righteousness, revealed throughout Scripture. God has a tender heart towards the oppressed and those unjustly treated. Scripture also reveals that God has very serious objections to those who seek to exercise ungodly power and control, and who oppress others. God's people should work to release the oppressed just as Jesus did!

4. God's Mission

Scripture reveals clearly that God is a missionary God who lives with purpose. God desires all peoples of the earth to know Him in relationship and worship Him, and He wants His kingdom established. He desires to share His purpose with all of His followers. All believers need to understand what is happening in the world and what still needs to be done. Jesus told His followers to "follow me." Therefore, all believers are to be World Christians.

5. God's Labourers

The task of the Great Commission is large and requires the gifts of all of God's people – both male and female. He has gifted both men and women and does not give gifts based on gender. Believers need to re-examine the difficult passages in light of these teachings.

Conclusion: Cast the Net!

If Jesus were to walk into your church or organization, would He say, "It is not good"? When was the first time God made this statement? In the Garden of Eden when man was alone! Or would God walk into your church or organization and see both men and women equally using their gifts, being trained to minister and lead, and would he say, "This is very good!" When is the first time God says this in the Bible? After He created the woman to stand beside the man as they shared equal blessing, dominion and responsibility!

The topic of unity among brothers and sisters in the Body is one of the greatest battles the Church must face. Because God's design was for men and women to serve side-by-side, Satan fights to maintain the hierarchy that places men over women. However, when the Church recaptures God's original intent, the unity will result in a great harvest of souls throughout the earth. Let us boldly cast the net of the kingdom!

5. Abuse and the Church

A. Abuse of Women
by Juliet Thomas

Introduction

In 1985, the song, "Dear Mr. Jesus" became a hit record. A nine-year old, reacting to a news report about child abuse wrote it.

> Dear Mr. Jesus, I just had to write to you; Something really scared me when I saw it on the news. A story about a little girl beaten black and blue. Dear Mr. Jesus, please tell me what to do. And please don't tell my daddy, but my mummy hits me too.
> [i]

Defining Abuse

Abuse has to do with "power'" and "powerlessness,'" with physical and mental injury, with vulnerability and violation, with fear and silence.

Gender-based abuse is endemic and affects women not only in the Third World but also women in every corner of the globe. Nor is abuse restricted to the rural, the poor and illiterate, but it is common among the urban, rich and educated. Sadly, it is also prevalent in the Church!

Physical violence is not the only kind of abuse. There are emotional, psychological, cultural, socio-economic, sexual, financial and even spiritual abuses. The problem of abuse is gaining more attention; it is also getting worse!

A Secular Perspective
1. Men as Abusers

Oppression and violence against women is the most ignored human rights issue, and, it is hurting evangelism.

Violence against women often receives social support. Neighbours, authorities and even the police hesitate to intervene because they feel abuse is a private domain. As a result, women are vulnerable to acts of violence in the family and in the community. Foeticide,

---

[i] Gary R.Collins, <u>Christian Counseling: A Comprehensive Guide</u> (USA: W Publishing Group, 1988), 309

infanticide, female genital mutilation, marital cruelty, dowry, murders, child abuse, incest and battering are forms of violence that women face in the family. At the community level women face the violence of rape, sexual harassment and sexual discrimination. Women also become the innocent victims of HIV/AIDS infection. Widow immolation, witch hunts, stripping and shaming of women, particularly those from the lower castes, often are used as punishment for their community's transgressions.

Abuse takes shape in the psyche of a human being. Abusers (often a man) believe that he is capable of doing harm to a person while being assured that he will receive social acceptance, that the family will remain intact, that the abuser will not be punished and that his share in the worldly affairs will remain intact. Institutions like the family, society and the Church, judicial systems and police are all responsible for cultivating and supporting this psyche.

The abuser subjects the victim to repeated accusations of provocation and destroys the battered woman's self-esteem causing a deep sense of shame and guilt.

Abusive behaviour can be learned from one generation to the next.[ii]

2. Women as Abusers
Abuse in a male-dominated society is carried on not only by men but also by women, whose loyalty towards men often perpetuates male violence on women. When men are accused of violence toward women, there are often women who defend the same guilty men. According to research by D. Albert, presented in Women's Link,[iii] he lists the following insights:

Women often close their eyes to violence done to other women by their close male relatives and associates. For example:
- A mother-in-law's oppressive behaviour towards a young bride.
- For all his crimes against humanity, Hitler had many female admirers and followers, obsessed with his destructive power.

[ii] Collins, 298
[iii] Alka Srivastava, ed., Women And Violence: Women's Link (New Delhi : Social Action Trust, 7:1 Jan-Mar 2001), 9-11

- Directly or indirectly, women are often women's own adversaries.
- A recent newspaper report, based on a survey, reported that 56% of women justify wife- beating.
- A mother's "step-motherly" treatment of her own daughter, particularly during her formative years, underscores the bitter truth that a mother is often unhappy when a female child is born, but dances for joy if she has a male child

When women's interests are thought to depend on men, they are known to approve, justify and endure male violence.

A woman's protective nature is well-known; she is like the proverbial mother hen that protects her chicks from all dangers even at the cost of her own life. But her protective nature assumes extreme forms when she feels compelled to shield her male family members, even when they are guilty of crimes against women.

Women in politics are easily co-opted into the patriarchal value system for gaining acceptability among their male colleagues.

Women are as cruel towards women as men are. Women are no different from men in their capacity for violent behaviour. The pity, however, is that the worst violence is often directed toward other women. They are loyal to their close male relatives and other associates because they have been inducted into a system that devalues women.

If violence toward women is to be redressed, women must radically evaluate their loyalty to men, as well as their own devaluation of women, in order to make better choices between loyalty that is just and legitimate, and one that is unjust and oppressive.

The Silence of Women Must Be Broken
Violence against women is a hidden evil in almost all societies. Many women are too afraid to share what they experience because they feel ashamed about what has happened to them. The problem often is that women do not want to humiliate those close to them by exposing their perpetrators. Psychological/emotional abuse, such as constant belittling, intimidation and humiliating treatment, also put women at risk for depression, suicide attempts, chronic pain syndrome and psychosomatic disorders.

Research by World Vision shows that women are often silent because they do not know what alternatives they have. Women dependent on spouses for income are afraid to leave the only form of security they know. Women are often forced into silence by fear of repeated or increased violence against them. Because of the violence done to their bodies and minds, women remain silent due to shame and humiliation.[iv]

Examples of Abuse in India:

- Millions of female foetuses are destroyed within the mother's womb.
- A teenaged handicapped girl in a local train in Mumbai is raped in full view of 5 male witnesses.
- Desperate mothers driven by poverty or forced by social and cultural pressure murder their girl babies soon after birth, by forcing scalding broth down the throat, or by feeding them the milk of a poisonous plant.
- A drunken husband, his spirit destroyed by drudgery and hopeless poverty, daily beats his wife violently, smashing her against the walls.
- Greedy in-laws and husband pour kerosene over a hapless, young wife, set her alight and claim it to be an accident or suicide – and go unpunished.
- Poor women devastated by flood and famine are forced to sell their girl children into prostitution for a hundred rupees.
- Even the police rape and sexually abuse women in their care. As reports of women's abuse are ignored, this often leads to the death of women.

Our system of education is male dominated. Education transmits traditional values and culture. Our traditional cultural values have subjected women to torture in the name of religious and cultural systems like widow burning and girl-child prostitution, female genital mutilation, etc.

Can an educational system evolved by patriarchy really liberate women? If women are to be liberated, it is possible only outside the

---

[iv] Don Brandt, ed., <u>Violence Against Women: From Silence to Empowerment</u> (Monrovia, CA: World Vision International, 2003), 85

formal system.[v] The gospel of Christ cannot tolerate such traditional cultural values.

We need to explore and give far more emphasis to the mental health aspect of abuse. This area has been largely neglected. The neglect may be explained by the social attitude of suppressing and ignoring factors regarding the inner life of individuals and families that are not easily classified as an 'illness.'[vi]

Understanding Self-Oppression
When dealing with abuse, we need to consider the emotional and psychological trauma caused to the inner life of the silent sufferer.

This negation and self-oppression of women becomes internalized and incorporated into one's view of one's self. We must battle this myth of powerlessness and fatalism and expose the lies and wrong assumptions, by countering them with the truth.

Lies Women Believe:
- There is something wrong with being a woman. There is something wrong with me.
- Sexual harassment occurs in so many subtle forms and with such frequency that it is a non-event and should just be accepted.
- There is no point in talking because nothing will ever change.
- If I talk about it, I'll be the one who gets the blame.
- Why talk? I won't be heard anyway.

Who embodies the 'truth' that can bring healing and wholeness to the abused woman's inner being? It is only Jesus! So, the Church must be God's primary tool of healing! Rehabilitation programs and secular strategies-no matter how good they may be - cannot bring the needed *shalom* to her whole being!

---

[v] Shashi Narayana, ed., Women And Education: Women's Link (New Delhi: Social Action Trust, 4:4 Oct-Dec 1998), 17
[vi] Shashi Narayana, ed., Violence Against Women: Women's Link (New Delhi: Social Action Trust, 5:1 Jan-Mar 1999), 8

How does the Bible address women's abuse? What is God is saying about women? Since Adam and Eve were created together in His image, what is His design and purpose, not only for women but also for men?

A BIBLICAL PERSPECTIVE [vii]

The remedy for abuse arises out of an emphasis noted at creation:

- Woman as God's image bearer.
- Man and woman together are called to reflect God's image.
- Both are created for relationship with God and one another.
- This is done effectively only in the context of community.

Abuse is a violation of all the above.

Woman as God's Image Bearer

Genesis 1:27 declares: *"And God created man (humankind), in His own image, in the image of God He created him; male and female He created them."* Unlike the other forms of His creation, God created humankind uniquely in His image. This humankind came as 'male' and 'female'. Both components were in Adam. When God took part of Adam to create Eve, he became predominantly male while she came to embody the female dimension of God. To express the fullness of God's image on earth, men and women must be reconciled.

What is God's image?

Genesis 1:26 tells us it is "according to His likeness" and normally we would understand this as God's moral character, and that He breathes His Spirit into us, bringing to life what we are; but it is more than this. To be 'in His image" includes three important factors:

1. God is a Trinity but one God. There is perfect unity and harmony within these three Persons. So as His "image bearer", male and female are meant to be 'one.' We are called to live together in harmony and unity.

2. The three Persons within the Trinity are one but different from one another. They are Father, Son and Holy Spirit. Likewise, though male and female are to

---

[vii] Ed Silvoso, <u>WOMEN God's Secret Weapon</u> (California: Regal Books 2001), 149

be as one, I personally believe that they are created different from each other, with different roles and functions.

3. The three Persons within the Trinity relate to one another in self-giving love.

Likewise, we are created and designed for relationships, primarily with God Himself, and equally important with one another in self-giving love. Our relationship with God is reflected in our relationship to one another. "Created in the image" of three self-giving, loving Persons of the Triune God, we are called to live in solidarity with others in the community, not for ourselves alone. In this community we derive our identities as husband, wife, brother, sister, etc. However, in a sinful world, we do not experience the ideal perfection that God intended in His original creation. Nevertheless, through our redemption in Christ we are restored and called to live again according to God's original design

Created in His image, humans were made for moral and fulfilling relationships with God, with one another, and with His creation. We become what God wants us to be only through nurturing and building relationships in community. There is no room for exploitative, abusive relationships within this community. God has not made us to be independent either of Him or of one another.

Women's abuse can therefore be defined as the violation and desecration of the sanctuary of God's image within the woman – not only her body which is the Temple of God – but spirit, mind, emotions – her very being. Jesus has come to set us free from everything that brings us into bondage.

Today we live in a fractured world, filled with abuse and barriers between people. The only hope for breaking down racial, caste and gender barriers lies in community. If there is true community, there will be equality – for men and women of every race and class and caste.

Unity means oneness. This means a total acceptance of each other and the commitment to build one another. There can be no second-class citizens. The unjust structures of society around us therefore should have no relevance inside the Church. The call is to overcome the worldly way of viewing gender, race and class. The following is from a friend in Turkey.

It is tragic to me that in a Muslim society where women are viewed as, might I say, 'second-class' citizens, the church also follows these same lines! This is presented as 'theological issues' that filters down to the way women view themselves, where they receive purpose and value and at what level they are considered a part of the church, both in their own eyes and the eyes of the men in the church.

For the sake of women, for the health and vitality of the whole church, local and universal, I believe we are holding back the church and growth of the kingdom because we are holding back the gifts of the Holy Spirit in the lives of women! In the Church, many of us are actually living in a "hierarchical or class system" to which Jesus Christ was so opposed!

Who is going to model community? Will government, or schools or businesses? No, only the Church can! It is urgent that the Church reclaim the Biblical model of community and begin to live it.

Gender and Men:
Gender is not only about women – but also about men. Empowering women is sometimes seen as disempowering men. This should not be so!

If women are to be major economic players in the churches and households, then men's roles must also change. When we encourage and develop women, changes must occur also in the structures within the family, the Church and the workplace. Without changes to the present structures, development and wholeness of women will remain only a dream!

The restoration of men is crucial to the eventual restoration of women.

The most warming example I saw of this was in talking to a small group of village women who had come for a women's empowerment program, in the city of Jabalpur. I asked them: "*Who is looking after your children and home while you are here?*" Very happily several voices answered together: "*Our Mr.*"

We sometimes see similar changes in the cities where women are engaged in demanding professions outside the home. Men begin to take a more active and positive role in caring for the children.[viii]

But sadly often this is not so in the Church. One highly qualified woman I know, who was much sought after, even by the government of the country for her input and expertise, said in despair: *"When I come home, I am nobody! And I am silenced in my church! I would have given my life to serve the church, but I am not allowed to speak or participate in anything!"*

This is spiritual abuse.

In the community, the rights and responsibilities of women and men are interdependent. That means both have to cooperate if gender-related discrimination is to be overcome. For these development activities to produce positive results, women and men should benefit equally and have equal power and influence.[ix]

In conclusion, we need to remember two things: First in considering the effects of abuse, we see that the victim is not the only one who suffers. Family members, boyfriends, associates of rape victims and close friends may all react with anger, confusion, prejudice and feelings of helplessness, revulsion and embarrassment. The Church and its mission will not escape suffering.

Second, we should not forget the abuser. In Christ we are called to love and seek reconciliation. According to counsellor/author Collins, often these abusers feel deep and lasting remorse, especially after their abusive behaviour becomes public knowledge. Many are frightened, guilt-ridden and find little support from others. Few attempt to understand abusers and to offer them much needed help.

Closing Appeal: Will the Church be Silent?

Today, especially from the Third World countries, "a cry is heard." Does the Church hear it? It is the cry that this new community, which is Christ's Body, called to show forth His glory, including justice,

---

[viii] Marianne De Nazareth, Who Won't Love This Man (Bangalore: Deccan Herald, Living, Dec 24, 04), 1

[ix] Heather Elliott, Gender and Development Global Future (California: World Vision International, Second Quarter 2003), 8

is not fulfilling its mission. Will the Church still be silent? Or will the Church hear and respond?

B. Strategies to Prevent the Abuse of Women
by Daniela Kurz

- How prevalent is abuse against women in secular and Christian cultures?
- What is a biblical response to the abuse of women?
- What strategies can we offer to prevent abuse?

Abuse against women in secular and Christian cultures shows itself in a variety of forms: sexual abuse, emotional abuse, abuse of power/influence and physical abuse. All four types of abuse occur in secular and Christian cultures. The estimated numbers of unknown cases is believed to be very high, due to the fact that even today we hardly discuss the topic of abuse.

I have observed a difference between secular and Christian cultures regarding the frequency of the four types of abuse. Yet it is important to acknowledge that all four types occur in both secular and Christian cultures.

The abuse of power/influence and emotional abuse are often more prevalent – yet sexual and physical abuse still occur in high numbers.

How do the four types express themselves? One of the most prevalent abuses, especially in Christian cultures, is the abuse of power and influence. In many cases, leaders abuse power to reach certain goals, to satisfy their own ego and to prevent others from gaining power. Often the abuse is not recognized nor discussed. Christian cultures seem to provide an open door for this kind of abuse and it has a devastating effect on world evangelism. Even Paul was astonished by it when he wrote to the Corinthians, "*For you bear with a man if he brings you into bondage...*" (2Corinthians 11:20). The victim is often not aware of the abuse and also filled with self-doubt.

In some Christian cultures, the abuser often uses false theology in abusive power against women. The issue of gender and giftedness is

87

often not discussed and many women are unsure of their own theological viewpoint. The abuser may demand love, patience, tolerance and humility. Many leaders have taught Christians that love, humility and understanding have no limits. They fail to explain that one can be abused in the name of love and tolerance. Another factor is that we Christians are often too passive and are unwilling to confront abuse in our churches. We have learned not to question or contradict those in positions of leadership or power.

In secular society, the abuse of power against women is often more obvious, yet often the victim is dependent on job and money and is therefore unwilling to confront the abuse. The weak economy supports abuse, because women are insecure and more willing to suffer for fear of losing their jobs.

There are several reasons we still have so much abuse. First, the topic is not really discussed in society. Second, we underestimate the dependency of women on their abusers. Third, our legal system is very complicated and requires much work for women to oppose their abusers.

In Christian cultures we often ignore the signs of abuse, because it is easy to ignore and we are afraid of the consequences of action. In the name of forgiveness, we deny the importance of the abuse and we are often more concerned with the image of the church than with the victims. This does not forward the gospel.

Further, there is often an underlying question about the possible guilt of the women themselves. It is important to understand that no behaviour on the part of the victim excuses the abuse. Another problem is that men and women who are not involved in abuse have a hard time understanding the victim or the abuser and therefore would rather not get involved.

What is a biblical response to the abuse of women?
The Bible does not tolerate abuse of any kind. Sometimes abusers hide their abuse under the name of discipline, but the Bible clearly teaches that discipline is inseparable from love. Each individual is loved by God and must be treated with respect and dignity. Love opposes abuse.

We need to ask the questions: "What can a church leader do to prevent abuse" and "where are the limits?" The church leader, according to the New Testament (1Peter 5:2), is to guide the people, as the shepherd does his sheep. If the leader uses his position to control and manipulate women, this must be viewed as abuse and a great detriment to the cause of Christ.

What strategies can we offer to prevent abuse?
1. Be open to discuss abuse. Provide a "room" for women to talk and discuss the topic. Create an atmosphere of honesty and reflection. Women need to know that they will be heard, that abuse is taken seriously and is a negation of the gospel.
2. Create a system of mentoring. Rehearse the truth that no one should have too much power and all are called to accountability.
3. Teach sound theology. The bible teaches we are all sinners! In addition to sound theology, we must also teach people to discern circumstances or to ask others to help them with discernment. People who are given the Spirit of discernment (1Corinthians 14:29) – are able not only to listen to the "good" words of others, but they are also guided by the Spirit to discern what is wrong.
4. We must name abuse by its true name and let truth be revealed. Further, people need to recognize consequences and not be afraid to discipline the abuser in a biblical way.

6. Reconciling our Different Views

A. Three Interpretations of What the Bible Teaches About Gender
by Kevin Giles

Evangelicals, committed to the permanent subordination of women, invariably claim that what they teach is what the Bible teaches. The truth is that what they teach is *one interpretation* of the Bible on this issue. Every attempt to give meaning to the words on the pages of our Bibles (or any other book) is an interpretative exercise. We only can have good, bad or indifferent interpretations of texts. There are in fact three well supported interpretations of what the Bible teaches on the status and ministry of women. What we have to decide is which one of these interpretations makes most sense of everything said in the Bible and of the key texts.

(i) The historical interpretation of what the Bible says on women, circa 200 AD to 1950
For long centuries Christian theologians (Tertullian, Chrysostom, Augustine, Aquinas, Luther, Calvin and the Puritans) interpreted the Bible to be teaching that God had made men "superior," women "inferior." There were no dissenting voices. They developed their doctrine of the sexes by reading the Bible through the grid of the cultural norms of their day. They interpreted the Bible as follows:

1. Man and woman are created by God but woman is created as man's subordinate helper. He is first/superior and she is second/inferior (Genesis 1 and 2). From the time of Augustine, it was generally thought that women do not fully bear the image of God (key text 1 Corinthians 11:7). Calvin said woman was created to be "*a kind of appendage to man.*"

2. Woman is responsible for the fall and sin (Genesis 3). She is the "*devil's gateway*" (Tertullian). For this reason she is more susceptible to sin and error. She needs the leadership of the more morally upright man.

3. The coming of Christ changes nothing. Women remain inferior to men.

4. Women should not hold leadership positions in any sphere. On 1 Timothy 2:12 Calvin said, *"The rule of women is an unnatural monstrosity."* Man is first/superior, women second/inferior in *every sphere of life.*

5. In public life women should keep silent, especially in church (1Corinthian 14:34, 1Timothy 2:11-12). In some church traditions, the absolute silence of women was demanded; in most they were allowed to sing hymns and say "amen" to the prayers.

What is implied in speaking of women as "inferior" is their ontological or personal inferiority. They lack something only given to man. Aquinas speaks of woman as a "defective male."

Comment

This understanding of what the Bible teaches on the sexes exactly reflected the cultural presuppositions of the theologians who gave these interpretations of the Bible. Because women were limited to the home sphere and excluded from education it was natural to think of them as inferior. Three theological problems with this approach are:

1. Genesis 1:27-28 says man and woman alike are made in the image and likeness of God.
2. Paul in Romans and Corinthians makes Adam responsible for the Fall (Romans 5:12 ff, and1 Corinthians 15:21).
3. In this schema Christ does not bring anything new.

The post 60's revolution

In the late sixties a social revolution erupted — the emancipation of women. Under the impact of this revolution all Christians have reformulated their theology of the sexes. It is hard to imagine that a theologian today would publicly argue that women are inherently inferior to men and more prone to sin and error. As a consequence, evangelicals have developed two novel competing and opposing theologies of the sexes. Both reject the central tenets of the historic position, yet their conclusions are very different. They both endorse the complementarity of the sexes but one sets men over women in a permanently fixed hierarchical order (the hierarchical-complementary position), the other places them side by side as social equals (the egalitarian-complementary position).

(ii) The contemporary hierarchical interpretation of what the Bible says on women

In response to this huge social change, conservative evangelicals committed to upholding male leadership in the church and the home, which they think is God-given, developed a totally new reading of what the Bible says about women. They called this at first the "traditional" or "historic" position and later, more euphemistically, the "complementarian" position. However, this interpretation of the Bible is completely novel. It is a break with what Christians for at least eighteen centuries had claimed the scriptures taught. In this post 70's reading of the Bible, the key texts are interpreted as follows.

1. Man and woman are both made in the image and likeness of God (Genesis 1:27). Genesis chapter 2 explains how they are differentiated. The man is made by God as the leader of the woman, indicated by the fact man is made first. He names the animals and she is made as his helper. The narrative of the fall in chapter 3 tells how the woman, who was to obey the man as her "head," usurped her subordinate "role" and acted independently. As a result, man's godly leadership of her becomes a burden and her distinctive womanly "role" is marred by painful consequences (Genesis 3:16).

2. Jesus treated women well, as all Christian men should treat women well, but he made it clear that only men could be leaders among God's people, as his appointment of twelve male apostles illustrates.

3. Paul teaches that the man is the "head" of the woman (1Corinthians 11:3) and the husband the "head" of the wife (Ephesians 5:23). Paul and Peter also exhort women to be subordinate to their husbands (Ephesians 5:22, Colossians 3:18, 1Peter 3:1). This is based on the unchanging created order. These texts clearly show that different "roles" have been given to men and women. The "role" of "headship" (in plain speak, leadership) is given to men alone.

4. Because the headship role has been given to men and men alone, husbands should lead in the home and men should lead in the church. Women in particular should not teach men (1 Corinthians 14:34-35, 1 Timothy 2:11-12).

5. What the Bible says on the leadership of men in the home and the church is based on one of the constitutive creation orders given before sin entered the world. This means that before the fall, God gave to men

and women "different roles"; the man is to command, the woman to obey. This teaching is universally binding and transcultural. The coming of Christ in no way annuls this creation order - it is the ideal.

6. None of the passing comments in the New Testament about women in ministry are of any great significance. All the cases cited speak only of women in subordinate ministries. Prophecy is totally distinct from teaching. It is not an authoritative proclamation, so the mention of women prophesying does not suggest a tension with 1 Timothy 2:11 that forbids women to teach.

7. The doctrine of the Trinity indicates that just as the Father rules over the Son, so men are to rule over women. The Trinity shows that personal equality and subordination in "role" can be reconciled. A subordinate "role" does not imply the inferiority of the Son of God or that of women.

8. To reject this Biblical teaching on "the role differentiation" of men and women is to reject the authority of the Bible. Those who argue for the equality of the sexes have assumed the non-Christian values of our age.

In this developed theology of the sexes, the biblical word "subordination" is avoided wherever possible and it is denied emphatically that this position implies any inferiority in women. When the word subordination is used, we are told all that is demanded is *functional* or *role* subordination; women's inherent equality with men before God is not being questioned.

Comment
This interpretation of the Bible's teaching on the sexes is novel in concept and wording; only the outcome is much the same. Never before in the history of the church has anyone suggested this is what the Bible teaches. It directly contradicts the historic or traditional interpretation of the Bible which concludes that men are "superior," women "inferior" and that women are more prone to sin and deception. Also contrary to historic position this post 1970's view interprets the Bible's teaching on sexual differentiation in terms of "role differentiation," not one's sexual identity given by God (Genesis 1:27-28), the story of the Fall (Genesis 3) as the sin of "role reversal", not disobedience to God's command and the fact that woman is created chronologically second as indicating the

existence of a permanently binding *social* order that gives pre-eminence to men. Let me spell some of this out in more detail.

1. Women are subordinated by a prescriptive social order given in creation. In the historic argument, there is no mention of a constitutive and prescriptive order of creation. Women are "inferior" because they were created second (chronological order). The whole idea that there are "orders of creation," social norms given by God, was first suggested in the 19th century. In this construct "orders of creation" covered the whole creation and were binding on all people, believers or otherwise (i.e. marriage and the state). They were contrasted with "orders of redemption" that applied only to Christians in the church and the home. How then can modern hierarchalists restrict women's subordination only to the home and the church, if they are claiming women are subordinated in a supposed order of creation? Are they not being inconsistent in applying their own theology? No answer is ever given to this question.

However, we must also ask, what in scripture suggests that in creation God established an unchanging and unchangeable social order in which men rule over women? If anything, the Bible suggests that in making men and women in his image, God gave them both incredible potential for leadership and change. In the Old Testament and in the history of the world, we see human beings changing social orders as history unfolds. How society is structured is always a human construct and as such, humans can change it, given the will to do so. There is no such thing as a God-given and unchanging social order. This idea is always brought forward by those in power in order to resist change. As far as the New Testament is concerned, the coming of Christ inaugurated a "new creation," which transcends the old or first creation (cf. 2Corinthians 5:17)

2. Women are equal with men: they simply have different roles. In the pre 1970's theological texts and commentaries, the word "role" or "function" is not mentioned. Women are in themselves "inferior" to men. Can you have *permanently fixed roles* that do not imply inferiority? If the roles are based on gifting or training and they can change, equality is not called into question, but if the roles are fixed and gender specific, then the perception of inferiority would seem inevitable. What is in fact being implied is that women are the subordinate sex. Their subordinate status is what defines who they are. The idea that men and women are differentiated primarily by roles is unbiblical. God creates us as men and women (Genesis 1:27). Our sexual identity is not determined by what we do (lead or not lead) but by who we are. This is, I am sorry to say, a fallacy. Hierarchalists are not arguing that men and women have different "roles" in the dictionary meaning of this word, so as to suggest women do certain things like cook and sew and men do other things. Only one issue is always in mind: *who leads and who obeys in the home and the church*. The true issue is *gender relations* (who exercises power) rather than *gender roles* (who should do the cooking, mow the lawns, pay the bills etc.)

Possibly the greatest problem this position raises is that it is unjust. It demeans women. They are excluded from sharing responsibility for the life of their church and their home simply because they are women - and it is claimed this is God's idea. Modern hermeneutics has raised the question of the morality of any interpretation. Who benefits and who is discriminated against by a particular interpretation?

(iii) The contemporary egalitarian interpretation of what the Bible says on the sexes

A second, novel interpretation of what the Bible teaches on the sexes also emerged in the post 70's period. Those who take this position argue that the historic or traditional interpretation of the Bible was in error. The Bible makes the equal consideration of women and men the God-given ideal. Comments about the subordination of women in scripture, like those on slavery, are practical advice to women living in a patriarchal culture that do not apply in our egalitarian culture. They read and interpret the Bible in this manner:

1. In creation, God made man and woman equal in dignity and status, giving them both authority to rule over the world (Genesis 1:28). Genesis chapter 2 teaches that men and women complement each other in their differentiation. The solitary "Adam" who is help-less and incomplete only truly becomes man differentiated from woman when man and woman stand side by side. This second creation story underlines the equality and differentiation of the sexes, not their hierarchical ordering. There is no subordination of the woman before the fall.

2. The subordination of woman is grounded in the Fall (Genesis 3:16). Only as a consequence of sin does woman find herself subordinated to man.

95

3. Jesus in His teaching and actions insisted on the equal dignity of men and women. Not once does He imply that women are subordinate to men, and He says and does much to imply the opposite. The Gospels depict Jesus as breaking with the old Jewish order and laws in very profound ways. He was new wine. The twelve apostles are all men because they are the counterpart of the twelve male patriarchs and their main work was to be "witnesses" - something forbidden to women in first century Jewish society.

4. Paul's teaching on the body of Christ allows for no devaluing of the ministry of women. Men and women may minister in the congregation as the Spirit empowers (Romans 12:3-8, 1 Corinthians 12 to 14, Ephesians 4:11-12). These theological statements about ministry should not be minimised or discounted. The Spirit, Paul insists, is gender indiscriminate in bestowing his grace gifts that produce ministry in the church.

5. In 1 Corinthians 11:3ff Paul speaks positively about men and women leading the gathered church in prayer and prophecy, the two most important ministries in that church. In 1 Corinthians 12: 28 Paul makes prophecy "second" only to apostleship and lists teaching "third." In 1 Corinthians 11, Paul's main concern is with sexual differentiation. Sexual differentiation does not imply subordination and never has.

6. In Ephesians 5:23 Paul calls the husband the "head" – in this instance using the word in the sense of "boss" – of the wife, but then he redefines what this headship implies. It is not leadership as this world knows but the leadership exemplified by Jesus in the incarnation. It is that of a servant who is willing to serve even to the point of giving one's life for the other. In Ephesians 5 Paul is seeking to transform patriarchy. When first read at Ephesus, this passage would have offended the men present, not the women as it does today. Not one word is said in this passage about who makes the final decision on matters of importance.

7. The exhortations to wives to be subordinate parallel the exhortations to slaves to be subordinate. Both are practical advice to people in the first century, not timeless precepts. *None of* these exhortations is based on appeals to the creation order.

8. The call to silence in 1 Corinthians 14: 34-35 is textually doubtful (see Fee and Payne), but if it is genuine, it only asks wives to desist from asking questions in church. The Timothy passage (1

96

Timothy 2:11-12) is the most difficult, but when set in the context of the debate about false teaching it would seem to be only forbidding certain women from teaching because they were involved in heresy. The use of the exceptional verb *authentein* suggests an exceptional situation. The two supporting comments drawn from the creation stories speak to the situation envisaged. Women are not to claim they should be "first," because remember Adam was created first and they are not to think they are above error because remember it was the woman who first fell into error. We see Paul arguing in a similar way in 1Corinthians 11:2-16 when demanding that women cover their hair. Here, too, he appeals to the creation stories, but virtually no one thinks women need to cover their heads in church today.

9. This reading of 1 Timothy 2 makes sense of Paul's many positive comments about the ministry of women. He speaks of a woman apostle (Romans 16:7), of women house-church leaders (Colossians 4:15 etc), of women prophets who spoke the word of God with authority (1Corinthians 11:4) and it seems he allowed women as a general rule to teach. They must have been doing this at Ephesus for some ten years before he asked them to desist in 1Timothy 2:11-12. The gifted women leaders Paul commends surely taught in the little house-churches of the first century. When these comments on the ministry of women are given the full weight they deserve, we see that Paul's inclusive theology of Spirit-given ministry is matched by his normal practice.

10. The thought that women are permanently subordinate because of a once given, permanently binding, transcultural order of creation is not taught in Genesis, and even if it were, the New Testament teaches that the new creation in Christ transcends the old creation (2Corinthians 5:17, Galatians 3:28). All that is mentioned in 1Timothy 2:13 is that "*woman was created second*." Calvin points out that this is not a very strong argument for women's subordination and I would agree. It states a fact. It prescribes nothing.

11. Rather than the doctrine of the Trinity supporting the subordination of women, it disallows it. The orthodox doctrine of the Trinity allows for no subordination in being or role for any of the persons in the eternal Trinity. See the Athanasian Creed. (Only in the incarnation does Jesus voluntarily subordinate himself to the Father.) In the historic debate on the differentiation of the three persons, their distinctiveness is based not on their differing roles but on their differing

relations. (The Son is the Son of the Father, the Father is the Father of the Son etc.) They work or function as one.

In this paradigm men and women complement one another by standing side by side. This position is to be contrasted with the hierarchical complementarian position where the man always stands over the woman. In other words we are all complementarians despite our profound differences over what this involves.

Comment
This reading of the Bible reflects the hermeneutical premise that a profound change in culture will often impact (not determine) how the Bible is interpreted. Today we no longer accept as an axiom that women are inferior, more prone to sin and error, and not equipped for leadership. With our new "spectacles" on, we see things in the Bible hitherto not seen and question old interpretations which it seems were determined by a patriarchal world view.

This position has the ability to make sense of the diverse teaching in scripture on the status and ministry of women. It allows for a harmonious reading of the Bible. What is more, it is just and fair. Men and women, differentiated by God, are both accorded the dignity and freedom demanded by their equal Godlike status given in creation. I suggest this is the best interpretation of what the Bible says on women and the one all Christians today should embrace.

B. "Can't We Just Be Friends?"
By Lorry Lutz

I spent an hour with a pastor of a mega-church that has several ordained women on its staff and a large number of women as elders. As I explained to him the purpose of this paper — to find ways to present our position to those who took a different view with love, understanding and confidence — he remarked, "I didn't think that was even an issue any more."

Why should we deal with reconciliation?

Unfortunately not only is the question of women in ministry still an issue, in some circles it is becoming more polarized, at least in the United States. For example, a church which does not ordain women or elect women elders recently removed the title "pastor" from key women on the staff, a title these women had held for some years, until a new pastor arrived. I personally felt a jolt when a friend of mine told me that when she was carrying a copy of my book about women as risk-takers, one of her friends noticed it. "Why are you reading that?" she questioned. "Don't you know she's a **feminist**?" (And I'm sure that was with a capital F!)

The literature of the complementarians (who believe in separate hierarchical roles for men and women) says that egalitarians are on a "slippery slope" and have "lost their biblical identity." Egalitarians, (who emphasize that in Christ men and women are not in a hierarchy) often express resentment and bitterness at the other side's stance.

These attitudes reflect disunity rather than love, rigid positions rather than a willingness to listen and have undermined the synergy that a vibrant Church needs in order to impact our sinful world. Jesus' prayer remains unanswered, "*May they be brought to complete unity to let the world know that you sent me.*" (John 17:23).

What basic issues do both sides agree on?

In spite of some opinions to the contrary, evangelicals on both sides hold to a basic core of faith including: the inspiration of Scripture as fully God's word; God as creator of the universe and of men and women equally in His image; the virgin birth, death and resurrection of Jesus, His atonement for our salvation and His Lordship in our lives; the Holy Spirit's power and indwelling. Those who hold to these teachings are certainly brothers and sisters in Christ. Respected leaders on both sides teach that marriage is between one man and one woman and that practicing homosexuality is sin.

Why do complementarians find it difficult to bridge the gap?

On the complementarian side, the most serious criticism is that egalitarians misuse Scripture. Complementarians maintain they use Scripture, while they feel egalitarians explain why Scripture doesn't apply. Other complementarians make more serious accusations that egalitarians hold "a worldview that is in conflict with the Scriptures."

Some complementarians believe egalitarians are dangerously dancing on the slippery slope towards approval of homosexual behaviour. They believe egalitarians use similar arguments to prove their case — that the prohibitions were only against special cultural situations. While egalitarians do point to some cultural specificity, as well as looking at scriptural context and the Scriptures as a whole on the subject, they point out that many complementarians themselves also reject portions of scripture as limited to biblical culture, e.g., wearing head coverings and the portions on slavery.

Complementarians believe that compromising with culture is the driving force that causes many women to step out of their roles as submissive wives and full-time mothers to search for the illusive rewards of career and independence. We are warned not to cave in to culture.

Why do egalitarians find it hard to reconcile with the complementarians?

Changes in society, which gave women opportunity for education, careers, leadership in business and government, also gave women the desire to be fully accepted and used in the church. Since the early 1900's when a missionary doctor, Katherine Bushnell, wrote *God's Word to Women,* hundreds of evangelical theologians and scholars have studied the Scriptures affecting women from a new paradigm. Yet complementarians generally are unwilling to accept the research as valid or even honest.

Egalitarian women tend to feel that ego, turf protection and authoritarianism cause male leadership to undervalue and under-utilize women's gifts. They point out how few boards, committees, and task forces include a proportionate number of women, even when these positions have nothing to do with questions of ordination or eldership.

Egalitarians fear that the misuse of authority in marriage can lead to abuse. They believe that certain teaching puts husbands on a guilt trip if they don't take a dominant leadership position in the home, rather than a mutually supportive one.

An interesting side note, as research confirms: In good marriages, whether complementarian or egalitarian, when husbands serve their wives out of love and encourage them to use their gifts, wives blossom; when wives serve their husbands by empowering and encouraging them, husbands grow.

Is it possible to "agree to disagree?"

Both egalitarians and complementarians have built biblical cases for their positions. Highly respected evangelical scholars and theologians on both sides have studied and researched the issue. These are men and women of integrity who honour the Word of God. Just as we have come to accept the scholarship and integrity of evangelical theologians who hold various interpretations of eschatology, can we not accept that there may be different interpretations of Scripture on the role of women? We are not dealing with a heaven/hell issue here!

Dr. John Stevens of the First Presbyterian Church in Colorado Springs argues, "There is a strong case for and against [women in leadership in the church.] The Bible is not uniformly in agreement. If it isn't clear, don't divide the church over it." Loren Cunningham, the founder of *Youth With A Mission*, states that the question of gender is "the leading subject in the Body of Christ and in the societies of the world today."[i] He also says, "As we release women, we'll mobilize the hundreds of thousands of people needed to complete the Great Commission. We'll see God's blessing on unity and servant leadership."[ii]

---

[i] Loren Cunningham and David J Hamilton, Why Not Women? (Seattle: YWAM Publishing, 2000), 235.
[ii] Loren Cunningham and David J Hamilton, 237.

History has two sides

Secular history weighs in heavily on male leadership in virtually every society. The writings of the Church Fathers reflect this patriarchy. For example, Origen, a third century North African scholar wrote, ". . . men should not sit and listen to a woman . . . even if she says admirable things or even saintly things; that is of little consequence since they come from the mouth of a woman."[xi]

John Chrysostom, a fourth-century theologian, wrote that God appointed different domains for men and women. The "more necessary and beneficial aspects to the man and the less important, inferior matters to the women."[xi]

Sadly, the church councils gradually lowered the status of women over the years. The Synod of Orleans in 533 abolished the office of deaconess "on account of the weakness of her sex." The Council of Tours later in the sixth century declared that women were impure by nature.

In spite of the fact that history is heavily influenced by patriarchal cultures and has buried the stories of great women leaders, women emerge in leadership in every stage of the church's history. New Testament house church leaders like Lydia and Phoebe reveal the important role women played. Paul greets 29 church leaders in Romans 16 — ten of whom are women, including Junia whom Origen himself honoured as a woman apostle. The twelfth century Hildegard of Bingen admonished her audiences to look to the Scriptures as their authority and to Christ, not the priests, for salvation. She was a woman before her time. And we haven't even begun to mention strong women leaders in modern times like author and teacher, Elizabeth Elliot, (a complementarian), or pastor and college president, Dr. Roberta Hestenes (an egalitarian.)

In the end it's a choice

Though he considers himself more a complementarian than an egalitarian, Pastor Ted Haggard, president of the National Association of Evangelicals, believes the Scripture leaves room for women in leadership. His own mega-church in Colorado Springs, New Life Church, has both male and female elders and ordains women pastors. However, his personal feeling is that men respond best to male leadership. He also admits that in the end it's a choice.

Those who choose the complementarian position do so because they believe that it is the plain reading of the Scripture, particularly in three main passages — 1Corinthians 11, Ephesians 5 and 1 Timothy 2.

Those who choose the egalitarian position believe that Jesus' radical view of women and the many models of women in leadership in Scripture describe a new paradigm. By studying the teachings and attitudes toward women throughout Scripture, and particularly Paul's partnership with women in ministry, they deal with the "problem passages" above within the context of the Scripture as a whole.

How do we reconcile when we've made different choices?
We should realize that this is part of a bigger issue.
1. *Theological:* The questions of biblical inerrancy and the eternal subordination of Christ to the Father are just some of the issues that complicate how we interpret the role of women in ministry.
2. *Culture:* The pressures of society on both men and women affect our views. While we cannot allow culture to determine what Scripture teaches, at times culture rightly forces us to rethink our interpretations. For example, society appropriately pressured the Church to rethink its position on slavery in the 19th century. However, the Church rightly resisted the pressures of the sexual revolution in the sixties. How much is culture or resistance to culture affecting how we resolve this issue?
3. *Gender differences:* Complementarians fear that men, because of their need for power, leadership and strength, will be emasculated by women in leadership. One pastor said, "It's not natural." Egalitarians may have to further study the unique natures of men and women, who in God's design complement each other to understand how to release and empower men in their God-given gifts.

We need to encourage open forums — but not debates.
• In her book, "The Argument Culture," secular sociologist Deborah Tannen describes our society. Rather than open dialogue where we listen to each other, we tend to take a position and learn how to defend it. She believes this is intensified by the male need to win rather than by the more relational way women look at things. While explaining our understanding of theology, these discussions need to be

fortified with personal experiences and anecdotes and a loving concern for the other person's needs.

- We should encourage these forums in each other's churches, in our men's and women's groups, and in our Bible studies, presenting both positions. It's important that we are assertive rather than aggressive and not angry or confrontational. We need to be well versed in our biblical position and not fear discussing an issue that seems controversial. Women may have to take the lead in these discussions because it means more to them personally.

We should be positive models for the world to see.

Those who are egalitarian need to develop and perfect the gifts God has given and be available to serve wherever God calls, sometimes even in a complementarian church. For all of us, we should never lose sight of the purpose for which God has gifted us – to advance His Kingdom and to do that with love and excellence, speaking the truth in love and working in partnership as men and women.

VI. CONCLUSION

We dedicate this Occasional Paper to those who seek to encourage and empower men and women to use their gifts to advance the Kingdom and do so in partnership. We celebrate the partnerships of men and women around the world who advance Christ's kingdom through life-changing, gospel ministries. We pray that our brothers and sisters will join us as we love and serve the Lord and as we continue to give careful consideration to the full development and deployment of men's and women's spiritual gifts, through prayer, dialogue and further study and reflection.

As an Issue Group we pray that our biblical, historical and social research, coupled with models of men and women in ministry will strengthen the gospel-partnerships of men and women working side by side. As we observe the sacrificial service and careful research of our scholars, evangelists and missionaries, we gain a clearer understanding of God's intention for Christian service through ministry partnerships. As Issue Group 24 we seek to equip the Church through our prayers and our ongoing work as a resource. May Christ advance the gospel through the gifts and humble service of all His servants.

VII. BIBLIOGRAPHY: FOR FURTHER READING

The following books, articles and Web resources provide additional information on issues related men, women and ministry.

Books

Alsdurf, James and Phyllis. Battered into Submission: The Tragedy of Wife Abuse in the Christian Home. Carol Stream, IL: InterVarsity Press, 1989.

Bauckham, Richard. Gospel Women: Studies of the Named Women in the Gospels. Grand Rapids, MI: Wm. B. Eerdmans, 2002.

Belleville, Linda, L. Women Leaders and the Church: Three Crucial Questions. Grand Rapids, MI: Baker Book House, 2000.

Bilezikian, Gilbert. Beyond Sex Roles. Grand Rapids, MI: Baker Book House, 2004.

Bristow, John Temple. What the Bible Really Says about Love, Marriage, and Family. St. Louis: Chalice Press, 1994.

Brown, Judy, L. Women Ministers According to Scripture. Kearney: Morris Publishing, 1996.

Bushnell, Katharine C. God's Word to Women: One Hundred Bible Studies on Woman's Place in the Church and Home. Minneapolis: Christians for Biblical Equality, 2003.

Cunningham, Loren and David J.Hamilton. Why Not Women? Seattle: YWAM Publishing, 2000

Fleming, Dr. Joy Elasky. The Think Again! Series on Women and Men (Volumes 1-8). Think Again: www.equalitydepot.com

France, R.T. Women in the Church's Ministry: A Test Case for Biblical Interpretation. Grand Rapids, MI: Wm. B. Eerdmans, 1995.

Gill, Deborah and Barbara Cavanass. God's Women Then and Now. Springfield, MO: Grace and Truth, 2004.

Giles, Kevin. The Trinity and Subordinationism: The Doctrine of God & the Contemporary Gender Debate. Downers Grove, IL: Inter-Varsity Press, 2002.

Grady, J. Lee. 10 Lies the Church Tells Women: How the Bible has been Misused to Keep Women in Spiritual Bondage. Lake Mary: Charisma House, 2000.

Grenz, Stanley J. and Denise Muir Kjesbo. Women in the Church: A Biblical Theology of Women in Ministry. Downers Grove,IL: Inter-Varsity Press, 1995.

Groothuis, Rebecca Merrill. Good News for Women: A Biblical Perspective of Gender Equality. Grand Rapids, MI: Baker Books, 1997.

Hull, Gretchen Gaebelein. Equal to Serve: Women and Men Working Together Revealing the Gospel. Grand Rapids, MI: Baker Book House, 1987.

Keener, Craig S. Paul, Women, and Wives: Marriage and Women's Ministry in the Letters of Paul. Peabody: Hendrickson Publishers, 1992.

Kroeger, Catherine Clark and Mary J. Evans, eds. IVP Bible Women's Commentary. Downers Grove,IL: Inter-Varsity Press, 2002.

Kroeger, Cathie & Nancy Nason-Clark. No Place for Abuse: Biblical and Practical Resources to Counter Domestic Violence. Downers Grove, IL: Intervarsity Press, 2001.

Kroeger, Catherine Clark and Richard Clark Kroeger. I Suffer Not a Woman: Rethinking 1st Timothy 2:11-15 in Light of Ancient Evidence. Grand Rapids, MI: Baker Book House, 1992.

McNally Jane, Berkeley and Alvera Mickelsen. Abuse of Christian Women in India and Remedy in 12 Biblical Studies on Equality of Men and Women. ISPCK, Delhi, 1999.

Meyers, Carol G.E. Women in Scripture: A Dictionary of Named and Unnamed Women in the Hebrew Bible, the Apocryphal/Deuterocanonical Books, and the New Testament. Grand Rapids, MI: Wm. B. Eerdmans, 2000.

Osburn, Carroll. Women in the Church: Reclaiming the Ideal. Abilene: A.C.U. Press, 2001.

Peirce, Ronald W. and Rebecca Merrill Groothuis, (General Editors.) Contributing Editor: Gordon D. Fee. Discovering Biblical Equality: Complementarity Without Hierarchy. Downers Grove, IL: Inter-Varsity Press, 2004.

Perriman, Andrew. Speaking of Women: Interpreting Paul. Leicester, England: Apollos, 1998.

Smith, Marilyn B. Lynn. Gender or Giftedness: A Challenge to Rethink the Basis for Leadership within the Christian Community. Manila, 2000.

Webb, William J. Slaves, Women, and Homosexuals: Exploring the Hermeneutics of Cultural Analysis. Downers Grove, IL: Inter-Varsity Press, 2001.

Articles

Bailey, Kenneth E. "Women in the New Testament: A Middle Eastern Culture View." Theology Matters. Jan/Feb 2000.

Bruce, F. F.   "Women in the Church: A Biblical Survey." <u>Christian Brethren Review.</u> 33, (December 1982), 7-14.

Christians for Biblical Equality's academic journal, <u>Priscilla Papers,</u> Volumes 7 to Present, available at www.equalitydepot.com.

Clinton, Robert J.   <u>Gender and Leadership, My Personal Pilgrimage.</u> Altadena, CA: Barnabas Publishers, 1995.

Gordon, A. J. "The Ministry of Women." 1894. (In Robert J. Clinton. <u>Gender and Leadership, My Personal Pilgrimage.</u> Altadena, CA: Barnabas Publishers, 1995.)

For   additional   articles,   books   and   resources   see www.cbeinternational.org

VIII. PARTICIPANTS

Convenor: Mimi Haddad **Co-convenors:** Lorry Lutz, Juliet Thomas
Facilitators: Esme Bowers, William Francis, Jo Anne Lyon, Eva Mrsic,
Kathy Oppenhuizen, Jessica Richards and Sarah Timarwa

First Name	Last Name	Country
Oluwakemi	Alabi	Nigeria
Lily	Chong	Malaysia
Dorothy	Colney	Myanmar
Jane	Crane	USA
Uma	David	India
Ellen	Duffield	Canada
Elizabeth Chidinma	Egbonuba	Nigeria
Joyce Winifred	Every-Clayton	Brazil
Kevin Norman	Giles	Australia
Florence	Grant	Australia
Norma	de Hernandez	Gautemala
David Joel	Hamilton	USA
Lana	Heightley	USA
Cosmas	Ilechukwe	Nigeria
Kamala	Jaggili	India
Daniela	Kurz	Germany
Helen	Loong	China
Cheryl	Lovejoy	USA
Judith	Mbugua	Kenya
Karen	Maczka	USA
Debbie	Menken Gill	USA
Geeta	Mondol	India
Rose	Mpuro Kamara	Uganda
Nora	Méndez	Venezuela
Dimitrina	Oprenov	Bulgaria
Russ	Palsrok	USA
Steve	Peace	New Zealand
Chad	Segraves	USA
Leslie	Segraves	USA
Cynthia	Stephen	India
Elke	Werner	Germany
Cecilia	Yau	USA
Beatrice	Zapata	Guatemala

List of Lausanne Occasional Papers from the 2004 Forum

Issue Group

No.	Topic	LOP No.
1.	Globalisation and the gospel	30
2.	The uniqueness of Christ	31
3.	The persecuted Church	32
4.	Holistic mission	33
5.	At risk people	34
6.	Hidden and Forgotten People	35
7.	Non traditional families	36
8.	Transformation of cities	37
9.	Partnership and collaboration	38
10.	The local church and evangelism	39
11.	Market place ministry	40
12.	Future leadership	41
13.	Prayer in evangelism	42
14.	The realities of changing expressions of Church	43
15.	The two-thirds world church	44
16.	Religious and non-religious spirituality in the post modern world	45
17.	Redeeming the Arts	46
18.	Evangelization of children	47
19.	Media and technology	48
20.	Understanding Muslims	49
21.	The impact on global mission of religious nationalism and 9/11 realities	50
22.	Confronting racial conflict and seeking Christian reconciliation	51
23.	Reaching the youth generation	52
24.	Empowering women and men to utilize their gifts for the spread of the gospel	53
25.	Making disciples of Oral Learners	54
26.	Reaching and mobilising the diaspora and international students	55
27.	Funding for evangelism and mission	56
28.	Effective theological education for world evangelization	57

* * *

These papers will be available as a Compendium published by William
Carey Library.
Online ordering at www.WCLBooks.com
Your can download one or more of these LOPs for personal use and see
other information on the Lausanne website at <www.lausanne.org>